Sea Survival
A Manual

Sea Survival

A Manual

DOUGAL ROBERTSON

 Praeger Publishers New York

Published in the United States of America in 1975
by Praeger Publishers, Inc.
111 Fourth Avenue, New York, N.Y. 10003

Library of Congress Card Catalog Number: 74–15683

ISBN 0–275–52760–3

CONTENTS

ACKNOWLEDGMENTS

I wish to thank the following people for their assistance in the compilation of this manual: Miss Lizzie Jackson for her secretarial work; Mrs Alison Quinn, my sister, who compiled the index; Surgeon Commander F. St.C. Golden for his assistance and permission to adapt the hypothermia diagram from the original; Arthur Littlewood for designing the Mariner's Compass rose; Eric Hosking for the majority of the bird photographs (those of the waterfowl, shearwaters, and fish were supplied by Bruce Coleman); R. K. Pilsbury, who provided the cloud photographs.

I owe acknowledgment also to the following organisations and publications for material and information: The Institute of Naval Medicine, Alverstoke; The Hydrographic Department of the British Admiralty; The U.S. National Oceanic and Atmospheric Administration (Environmental Data Service and The Smithsonian Institute); *Survival in Cold Water* by W. R. Keatinge (Blackwell 1969); *The Migration of Birds* by Jean Dorst (Heinemann 1962); *Birds of the World* by O. Austin and A. Singer (Hamlyn 1968); *Fisheries Oceanography* by Taivo Laevastu and Ilmo Hela (Fishing News (Books) Ltd. 1970); *Life and Death in a Coral Sea* by Jacques Yves Cousteau (Cassell 1971); *The Nautical Almanac*; Journal of the Royal Naval Medical Service.

D. R

LIST OF ILLUSTRATIONS

Drawings by Pam Littlewood

1 PREFACE

Disaster at sea seldom strikes in the same way twice. The circumstances and consequences of catastrophe are so variable that no hard and fast rules can be formulated to cope with the unknown factors of the situation. Safety routines carried out in the safe environs of an undamaged craft, while adequate for checking the working efficiency of materials and their usage, may be quite impracticable in disaster conditions. It is therefore of first importance that safety equipment should be either self-operating in the nature of their release mechanism or should at least be operable with a minimum of manual work by uninformed and unpractical people.

It is not, however, the purpose of this manual to investigate safety practices or appliances, a subject which should be dealt with quite adequately in the official publications of the relevant authorities. Its purpose is to provide survivors with enough information to enable them to cope with the life-and-death circumstances in which they find themselves immediately after their parent craft has sunk, and during the subsequent period of time which has to elapse before they reach safety either by rescue or by their own efforts, or, as is more usual, by a combination of both.

Information is a major factor in successful survival, and although survivors can learn much from their own mistakes, death may intervene before the learning can be applied to a second chance. Absence of, or bad, information can be as deadly as any other factor which may threaten the lives of castaways, so that those who find themselves in a survival craft and isolated from outside help should immediately study the information in this manual and their position on the charts contained in the back pocket, before deciding on any long-term course of action.

The information contained in this manual has been gathered mainly from three sources: the expertise which has been acquired and contributed by generations of seamen and scientists to contemporary nautical knowledge; the extensive and valuable research of practical survival institutes; and personal survival experience. The first two sources are self-explanatory and I would like to express here my deep appreciation for the encouragement and special help given to me by the Institute of Naval Medicine, Portsmouth, the staff of the Meteorological Office, Bracknell, and of Leith Nautical College.

The third source perhaps requires a little more explanation, for my main survival experience was thrust upon me in the Pacific Ocean when an attack by killer whales upon my schooner resulted in her sinking in 60 seconds, a thousand miles from the nearest practicable landfall. The story of the subsequent 37-day ordeal by six castaways, with emergency water and rations for only three days, is told in *Survive the Savage Sea* (Elek, 1973). It was this experience which brought home to me the importance of having available a manual which contains the information which castaways need to know, not only to survive the immediate emergency after the disaster but also to provide the data and advice which are necessary to their continued survival in long ordeals. My experience as a Master Mariner, as a hill farmer, and as an ocean yachtsman, has possibly made it easier for me to concentrate more readily on the issues at stake than if the subject was approached from a more academic standpoint. If I have dwelt on the basic principles of survival practice to the seeming exclusion of the more sophisticated aids provided by modern medicine and technology it is because these aids are not usually available in survival conditions.

I have no words to offer which may comfort the reader who is also a castaway, except that rescue may come at any time but not necessarily when you expect it; and that even if you give up hope, you must never give up trying, for, as the result of your efforts, hope may well return and with justification. You can expect good and bad luck, but good or bad judgment is your prerogative as is good or bad management, and it is in the exercise of the last two qualities that this book is designed to assist, and in assisting, influence the first in your favour.

2 URGENCY NOTES

The following is a summary of the survival action to be taken after the decision to abandon ship has been made.

(1) Abandoning Ship

Release survival craft. Send radio SOS to include position. Dress warmly to include waterproof outer clothing with life-jacket over. Collect additional water supplies. Try to enter survival craft without getting wet, especially in cold weather. Take supplementary fishing equipment food buoyancy. Keep survival craft clear of sinking ship and dangerous wreckage.

(2) Action in Cold Water

(a) *For survivors*

(i) Enter cold water fully clothed with waterproof outer garment and lifejacket, with whistle if possible.

(ii) When immersed in cold water remain as still as possible until rescuers come to you. Initial discomfort will decrease quickly.

(iii) Do not exercise to keep warm. Increased circulation will only accelerate loss of heat from your body.

(iv) Exhaustion will immobilise you very quickly in cold water; secure yourself to any necessary material or reserve flotation before this happens.

(v) Cold injury will not affect you before hypothermia. There is no need to take priority measures to counteract this form of injury.

(vi) If you have no lifejacket, secure yourself to other reserve buoyancy if possible.

(*b*) *For rescuers*

(i) If survivor is unconscious and not breathing. Note probability of drowning from posture in the water. Apply mouth-to-mouth respiration. Do not stimulate circulation by rubbing or by applied warmth, particularly if the casualty is very cold. Allow recovery to take place slowly in normal temperatures.

(ii) If survivor is unconscious and breathing slowly. Do *not* apply mouth-to-mouth respiration. Strip off wet clothes by cutting. Place survivor in unwarmed but dry insulating bag. Leave to recover without further assistance or interference (except if 'buddy warming' technique described on page 16 is implemented) unless breathing stops. The survivor may be assisted to rewarm only after consciousness is regained. It is of the utmost importance that very cold and unconscious survivors should be disturbed as little as possible. *Clinical assistance should only be given where expert care is available.*

(3) Action in All Waters

Bind wounds and look out for sharks and other dangerous fish. Strike them if they come near enough but do not splash the surface of the sea in an attempt to frighten them away as this is more likely to be interpreted as a distress signal, which will stimulate attack. Maintain contact with other survivors and secure yourself to any useful flotsam which will assist the survival of others or which may be used to ward off predators.

(4) Action on Boarding Survival Craft

Assist other survivors to board and secure useful flotsam. Attend to injuries, and if in cold areas, guard against onset of illness or injury from cold; examine inflatable raft for leaks and guard against excessive leakage of carbon dioxide gas into an unventilated raft. If there is more than one raft, secure them to each other. In rough weather, fit tension buffers to sea-anchor lines and also to lines joining rafts; this should be done with the minimum of delay to avoid damage to flotation chambers. Post lookouts to guard against dangerous wreckage. Anti-seasickness pills should be administered before seasickness starts, to avoid loss of body fluid. If castaways are already seasick administer suppositories if available.

Assess further action only after very careful consideration of all the factors involved. These must include the likelihood of search and rescue, position with reference to ocean currents and proximity to shipping lanes. The decision you are faced with at this time is the most important in your life; it should be taken only after full consultation with all the survivors and with the help of the best available information.

3 DISTRESS SIGNALS

INTERNATIONAL REGULATIONS
FOR PREVENTING COLLISIONS AT SEA

Rule 31

Distress Signals

When a vessel or seaplane on the water is in distress and requires assistance from other vessels or from the shore, the following shall be the signals to be used or displayed by her, either together or separately, namely:

(i) A gun or other explosive signal fired at intervals of about a minute.

(ii) A continuous sounding with any fog-signal apparatus.

(iii) Rockets or shells, throwing red stars fired one at a time at short intervals.

(iv) A signal made by radiotelegraphy or by any other signalling method consisting of the group ... — — — ... (SOS) in the Morse Code.

(v) A signal sent by radio-telephony consisting of the spoken word 'Mayday'.

(vi) The International Code Signal of distress indicated by NC.

(vii) A signal consisting of a square flag having above or below it a ball or anything resembling a ball.

(viii) Flames on the vessel (as from a burning tar barrel, oil barrel, etc.).

(ix) A rocket parachute flare showing a red light.

(x) A smoke signal giving off a volume of orange-coloured smoke.

(xi) Slowly and repeatedly raising and lowering arms outstretched to each side.

NOTE. Vessels in distress may use the radio-telegraph alarm signal or the radio-telephone alarm signal to secure attention to distress calls and messages. The radio-telegraph alarm signal, which is designed to actuate the radio-telegraph auto alarms of vessels so fitted, consists of a series of twelve dashes, sent in 1 minute, the duration of each dash being 4 seconds, and the duration of the interval between two consecutive dashes being 1 second. The radio-telephone alarm signal consists of two tones transmitted alternately over periods of from 30 seconds to 1 minute.

The use of the foregoing signals, except for the

purpose of indicating that a vessel or a seaplane is in distress, and the use of any signals which may be confused with any of the above signals, is prohibited.

Visual distress signals call the attention of passing ships, aircraft or coastal watchers to the plight of the survivors. A great deal of expertise has gone into the manufacture of pyrotechnic signals of distinctive and easily detectable pattern so that they will function efficiently in severe weather conditions with a minimum of effort, but no amount of skill on the part of the manufacturers can make a visual signal effective if nobody is looking. Modern ships have autopilots for helmsmen, radar scanners for lookouts and if it is the castaway's misfortune to encounter a vessel that has no proper lookout the chances are that his distress signal will burn out unseen.

(1) In the Day

It is of some use, therefore, to try to attract attention in daytime by a *heliograph*, or by making black smoke, so that a casual onlooker may be watching when the distress signal is actually fired. For the same reason, it is better for a hand flare to be fired before the discharge of a rocket flare, especially at night. The orange smoke of distress flares is sometimes difficult to see from a distance, especially in quick dispersal conditions, but a source of black smoke is usually investigated by a watchkeeping officer or perhaps an off-watch crew member with binoculars. Thus, in addition to the regulation distress flares, emergency kits should contain a means of making *black smoke* as well. A small bottle of paraffin sprinkled over surplus rubber material, tied to a paddle, lighted, and held to leeward of a raft may suffice. This also makes an effective night distress signal (except in areas such as the China coast, where this is a customary ·

method used by junks to warn ships of their presence). *Water dyes* are very useful for attracting the attention of searching aircraft, but are not included in many survival packs.

(2) At Night

Attracting attention at night is easier because flares can be seen over much greater distances. Distress rockets and hand flares can be visible in excess of 20 miles and torch signalling at 5 miles. When using the Morse SOS, due regard should be given to the height of the swell and whether the signal can be seen from a passing vessel when the survival craft is in the trough. Such signals should be slow and regular in calm weather, but in heavy seas an attempt should be made to transmit the full SOS while on the crest of the wave, otherwise the light may be mistaken for a small boat's navigation light dipping behind the waves.

Some form of *sound apparatus* (a whistle or horn) should be available to enable the castaway to attract the attention of unseeing ships on their close approach. The shouts of drymouthed weakened castaways do not carry very far but even so, these have been responsible for rescue being effected when all visual means had failed.

Many types of *radio apparatus*, in the form of beacons, or small radio-telephones, are now available in survival packs. *Radio-telephones,* though more expensive, have the advantage of providing two-way communication over longer distances than *beacons*, which have a very limited range (about 20 miles) to searchers at sea level but up to 200 miles to searching aircraft. Both beacons and radio-telephones are made to function automatically on distress frequencies and in the case of radio-telephones, transmission may be interrupted to broadcast a distress message and receive acknowledgement if communication is established.

Radio transmissions are usually limited by reserves of electrical energy, which, particularly on radio-telephones, is quickly exhausted if continuous transmission is maintained. Some energy should be kept in reserve to assist search and rescue craft to 'home' in on an RDF bearing.

4 PROCEDURE ON ABANDONING SHIP

While it is vital that survivors suffering from injury, near-drowning, immersion hypothermia or cold injury be brought aboard the survival craft as quickly as possible and given immediate care (see pp. 10–19), it is also of paramount importance that any debris floating nearby should be scrutinised and, if of the slightest possible use and not dangerous to the survival craft, be secured alongside or brought aboard, depending on the permeability of the material. The lives of the uninjured as well as the injured can sometimes depend on pieces of flotsam saved at this time. Materials to avoid are those with sharp edges, which could be dangerous to inflatable craft; heavy materials (spars, etc.) should not be tied alongside rigid survival craft where they could cause hull damage but may be secured to the sea anchor by a separate line to float clear of the survival craft. Foresight at this stage is all important, for damage sustained as the result of a thoughtless action may shorten the effective life of the survival craft and this can mean the difference between life and death.

Any buoyant materials should be secured in a safe place regardless of their apparent uselessness at the time; reserve buoyancy and waterproof container space are the castaway's two most precious assets, followed by shelter and warm clothing in cold areas, shade in tropical zones. Additional water reserves are vital in all climates.

Painters should not be secured to any part of the parent craft which is strong enough to allow the raft or boat to be dragged down with the sinking vessel before survivors have time to cut free. Additional stores should be secured to rafts or survivors by lines until they can be brought inboard. If the choice is available, it is better to lie to leeward of a sinking vessel, where some shelter may be gained while picking up survivors and where useful flotsam will drift down wind after the vessel has sunk. The danger of a wind-driven hulk drifting down on a survival craft can be met by fending off. If you have to enter the water without the prospect of reaching a survival craft it is better to go over the weather side where the hulk will not drift down on top of a swimmer.

If the parent craft is sinking rapidly, survival craft should be moved far enough away to ensure their safety. Safe distances depend on the nature of the disaster: for instance, there may be a danger of explosion or burning embers may cause damage to inflatable craft. Waves caused by capsize and suction from large vessels present a hazard to a survival craft as do buoyant materials breaking free from the sunken vessel and moving swiftly to the surface. Damage to inflatables can result from severe abrasions from the barnacled side of the parent craft and all survival craft are in danger, on the weather side of a ship, of being smashed or punctured beyond repair.

Wind-driven survival craft travel faster than burning oil unless they are well sea-anchored, but if it is necessary to swim through burning oil, swim to windward, using the breast stroke to sweep the flames aside. In intense heat it may be necessary to swim underwater, rising to the surface only to breathe, in which case a lifejacket and bulky clothing cannot be worn.

5 SURVIVAL IN WATER

(1) Drowning

Drowning is the most common cause of death at sea, and the most effective resuscitation treatment in survival conditions is the mouth-to-mouth method of artificial respiration (see diagram below). If the breathing has stopped, the casualty should be laid flat, face upwards with the head tilted back. Remove any obstructions from inside the mouth (such as false teeth) with as little disturbance as possible. If the throat is obstructed by mucus clear this by sucking or blowing if possible. Open the casualty's mouth, pinch his nostrils and

Mouth-to-mouth artificial ventilation (the position of the right hand is important)

placing your mouth over his lips, blow air into his lungs, noting the effect of this by the expansion of the chest. (If the mouth is injured, air may be blown through the nostrils while the mouth is covered.) Then allow the patient's lungs to exhale. Repeat this routine two or three times in quick succession, then continue at a steady rate of one breath every 6 seconds, but more slowly if the body is very cold.

The patient may try to vomit. If so, turn him face down immediately to prevent the vomit from entering the lungs, then resume mouth-to-mouth respiration until breathing is restarted. He should then be placed in the coma position, on his side, head to one side, one knee and one elbow at right angles (see diagram, below) to support him until recovery is assured.

The mouth-to-mouth method of artificial respiration does not interfere unduly with the slow recovery treatment for hypothermia (see below), although if the patient is very cold he should be disturbed as little as possible while being treated for drowning. When the patient regains consciousness his recovery can be assisted by giving him warm glucose drinks (the fluid should be warmed against another survivor's body if no other way is possible). Tolerable quantities of bicarbonate of soda in tepid water can be usefully drunk at this time.

(2) Hypothermia

The danger to life from cold, both in the acute form experienced from immersion in cold water, and the more prolonged

Coma position (the head should be lower than the feet)

type resulting from exposure and exhaustion in cold climates, is one of the greatest the castaway has to overcome.

If the disaster has taken place in an area where sea temperatures are below 20°C (68°F), the survivor faces the risk of becoming disabled due to a drop in deep body temperature and of dying from cold (hypothermia). The probability increases as the water temperature drops and the immersion period lengthens. There are ways in which human resistance to cold can be encouraged and the survivor's life prolonged, both by correct action of the survivor and the correct after care given to him by his rescuers. Instinctive first aid action of applied warmth or the stimulation of blood circulation in both situations is usually inappropriate and hastens the onset of unconsciousness and eventual death.

If time allows before abandoning the parent craft, survivors should try to dress as warmly as possible, preferably with an outer garment which is waterproof, before putting on their lifejackets and entering the water. If time is short, the waterproof garment should be first choice, with lifejacket over. If a survival craft is nearby, swim to it and get out of the water as quickly as possible. If there is no survival craft within reach, swim only far enough to clear the disaster area and then lie still; this has the twofold advantage of keeping blood circulation to a minimum (thereby preventing heat loss from the centre of one's body) and also of preserving the layer of warmer water inside one's clothing next the skin. The distance which people can swim in very cold water decreases sharply as temperature drops, so that in cold conditions they should keep as still as possible until the survival craft comes to them. Those not wearing lifejackets should avoid swimming in very cold water (less than 10°C) by clinging to some form of support, ie flotsam of any description, until rescued. It is important to remember that even expert swimmers quickly become exhausted and drown after a few minutes of swimming in very cold water. Survivors in cold water seeing rescue close at hand have left the safety of floating wreckage and have failed to swim to rescue craft, resulting in their deaths while trying to cover distances under 100 yards.

When survivors are rescued from cold water the action taken by the rescuers is vital to the life of the survivor.

SYMPTOMS AND SIGNS IN ACUTE HYPOTHERMIA

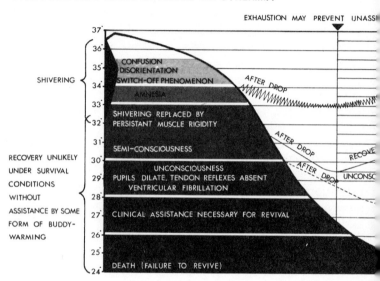

The curve represents the behaviour of body temperature during cold water immersion with the associated signs and symptoms encountered at the various body temperatures. When exhaustion is present in hypothermia (likely in prolonged ordeals or when vigorous exercise was necessary for survival), the victim's energy reserves may be so depleted that shivering will not resume on recovery, even when the indicated deep body temperature has been reached through assistance by buddy warming. If consciousness is regained without the resumption of shivering, buddy warming should be continued until energy reserves can be replenished by drinks. It is, however, important to remember that buddy warming in cases of deep hypothermia should be very minor, aimed at stopping further heat loss rather than promoting rapid heat exchange which may be harmful. Treatment

Generalisations are difficult to apply to the treatment of hypothermia but, if no civilised amenities are available, it is best to insulate the survivor from further heat loss and allow him to recover slowly, aided only by his own body

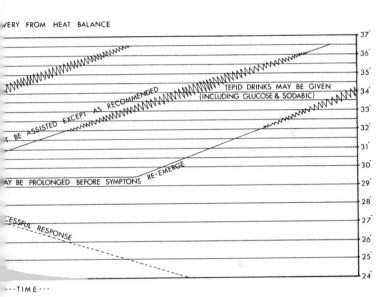

VERY FROM HEAT BALANCE

TEPID DRINKS MAY BE GIVEN
(INCLUDING GLUCOSE & SODABIC)

T BE ASSISTED EXCEPT AS RECOMMENDED

AY BE PROLONGED BEFORE SYMPTONS RE-EMERGE

ESSFUL RESPONSE

···TIME···

should also aim at eliminating further heat loss from wind chill, from contact with wet clothing, or by conduction to the floor.

APPROXIMATE TIME SCALE FOR SURVIVORS OF AVERAGE BODY BUILD

Temp. of water		Clothed	Unclothed
5°C	Survivor remains able for	60 mins	20-30 mins
10°C	Survivor remains able for	3 hours	1 hour
15°C	Survivor remains able for	5 hours	2 hours
20°C	Survivor remains able for	8 hours	4 hours

Thin survivors become helpless in a shorter time than those quoted; fat survivors, if warmly clad, remain able over much longer periods

warmth. Any artificial stimulation of blood circulation, either by exercise or applied warmth, to an unconscious survivor, far from helping, is more likely to kill him by assisting the cold blood near the surface of the body to return too quickly to the heart, thus causing a further steep drop in deep body temperature. This further or after drop often results in hypothermic survivors losing consciousness after they have been rescued. The symptoms displayed by survivors suffering from hypothermia become more acute with increase in time, succeeding each other more quickly as the water becomes colder, and are as follows: shivering, accompanied by confusion and loss of awareness, followed by amnesia. (see diagram, p. 14). As the survivor becomes semi-conscious, shivering lessens and is replaced by muscular rigidity. The final lapse into unconsciousness is accompanied by eye pupil dilation and generalised muscular relaxation simulating death very closely. If the heat loss is not stopped and reversed before this stage, recovery is further impeded by changes in blood chemistry; the survivor's heart-beat becomes erratic and death results from cardiac arrest due to the body's inability to function properly rather than from any particular injury due to cold. For this reason, where expert hospital care is quickly available, attempts at revival are successful in those who appear to be dead.

In a survival craft, however, no such assistance is available and expert opinion differs on the best recommended treatment. It would appear that the casualty who has gone beyond the shivering stage will, in all probability, die anyway unless some positive action is taken and the practice of 'buddy warming' would appear to be the only practical way of rendering assistance in such circumstances. The loss of body temperature in a semi-conscious or unconscious casualty may be counteracted to a certain degree by this method, which consists of a close approximation of two or more bodies hugging the victim, thereby increasing and assisting the available recovery powers, and at the same time reducing the overall area from which heat may be lost. As soon as the casualty has stopped losing heat, he should be allowed to rewarm without further assistance from buddies.

When such a technique is used aboard a survival craft care has to be taken that the buddies of the casualty do not themselves become cold to a dangerous degree and a close watch should be kept on them to guard against this. For the same reason, it is advisable for buddies to retain their clothing (apart from any outer insulating layers) rather than to try to promote rapid heat exchange by naked contact, which while helpful in preventing the onset of hypothermia in others, may have adverse consequences on those who are already hypothermic (see p. 16). If buddy warming is not practicable, then insulate the patient's body in a polythene bag if available, and place him in the coma position with the head lower than the feet. Guard against choking on fluid, and keep the temperature under the raft canopy or around the exposed area of the patient's body at an ordinary comfortable temperature. (In crowded rafts with enclosed canopies, quite high temperatures can be attained, even in cold climates, which would endanger the life of an unconscious hypothermic survivor.) Do not give any alcohol. Glucose in tepid water could assist recovery if the patient regains consciousness, and at this stage tolerable quantities of bicarbonate of soda may also be helpful. Warm drinks (from self-warming-type tins) would help, but make no attempt to administer such drinks to an unconscious survivor since this could result in death from heart failure, apart from the obvious risk of choking.

In conditions where survivors have to endure continuous exposure to cold wet weather over long periods in an open boat, the weaker and/or thinner castaways will be the first to show signs of chronic hypothermia. This may take the form of diminished shivering, accompanied by withdrawal or dissent, followed by, as in the more advanced stages of hypothermia, cessation of shivering and collapse. In such weather conditions, survivors should huddle together as much as possible, the boat should be 'hove to' under a sea anchor, and all energy conserved until weather conditions improve. Survival rations will not allow the most willing of castaways to expend energy needlessly, and the husbanding of strength and prevention of hypothermia or cold injury in such conditions are the most important acts of survival.

(3) Drowning or Hypothermia?

Although the most frequent cause of death at sea is undoubtedly drowning it should not be assumed that anyone rescued from the water in an unconscious or apparently dead state has in fact drowned.

Deep hypothermia can have symptoms of death and is difficult to diagnose even when clinical facilities and professional opinion is available. As the relatively inactive treatment advocated for hypothermia contrasts with the positive treatment for drowning, general guidelines only can be laid down to help the prescribed treatment.

(i) Lifejacketed casualties, semi-conscious, unconscious or apparently dead, should be assumed to be suffering from hypothermia and treated accordingly.

(ii) All others in an immersion state should be treated for drowning.

It is also probable that survivors who have been immersed in cold water (under 10°C) for over an hour or in not so cold water (10°C to 20°C) for several hours, and are unconscious, will be suffering from some degree of hypothermia, even if drowning is apparently the main cause of collapse; resuscitation should take into account treatment for both conditions. If an apparently drowning person loses consciousness after rescue and is also very cold, treat for hypothermia immediately while checking other symptoms.

Rescuers should bear in mind that the time spent on administering artificial respiration to a casualty suffering only from hypothermia could mean a fatal delay in the administration of the correct clinical treatment, if it was available. Drowning should therefore be correctly diagnosed in cold water immersion, and the length of time the casualty has been exposed to cold will be a significant factor.

It therefore follows that:

(i) Dangerous hypothermia is unlikely to be present in short periods of immersion.

(ii) Drowning takes place quickly with non-swimmers.

(iii) Good swimmers quickly become exhausted in very cold water, if they do not lie still, and may drown before becoming hypothermic.

(iv) Good swimmers falling unexpectedly into very cold water may inadvertently inhale a large quantity of water and drown immediately.

(v) The practice of taking several deep breaths immediately before an underwater swim can result in the instant drowning of a good swimmer.

On the other hand, drowning as the result of exhaustion or unconsciousness from hypothermia occurs after a much longer period and then usually to people supported by life-jackets or on wreckage. Only immediate hospital treatment can offer hope of resuscitation in such cases, but artificial respiration should be tried if death is not firmly established.

(4) Non-Freezing Cold Injury

Constant cold, associated usually with wet or immersion conditions in holed rafts or boats, results in cold injuries to limbs which can cause lasting damage to the limbs involved. The criteria for cold injury are as follows: (i) temperature less than 11°C; (ii) inadequate circulation due to cold, an inability to move, constriction of clothing, or any combination of these; (iii) wetness from any cause. The onset of cold injury may be detected by a feeling of numbness in the part affected later followed by a general swelling of the limb and discoloration. While in a raft or boat, in cold weather, the castaway should carry out exercises of the limbs, particularly the toes, at frequent intervals to maintain circulation, especially when numbness is felt, for prevention is the only effective cure in survival conditions. Do not use massage to stimulate circulation where numbness exists in cold injury.

There is no danger that this type of cold injury will develop in the relatively short space of time required to produce immersion hypothermia so that keeping still to delay the onset of hypothermia will not result in cold injury.

(5) Freezing Cold Injury

Cold injury from freezing, well known as frostbite, is recognised by the dead, white, frozen appearance of the part affected. Those most vulnerable to frostbite are lookouts on rafts and lookouts and helmsmen on boats, especially when low environmental temperatures are combined with air movement. The parts of the body most likely to be affected are nose, cheeks and fingers. In severe conditions, unprotected skin (hands, feet, etc.) will also be affected. Like its non-freezing counterpart prevention by early recognition is the best treatment. Lookouts should be warned of the danger and told to wrinkle nose and cheeks frequently and if sensation is lost, treatment should be begun immediately. Once frostbite is incurred, the part affected should be rewarmed as quickly as possible and then kept covered to avoid refreezing. Rewarming should take place by placing warm hands, or breathing, on the frostbitten part and not by rubbing; it should then be left to recover on its own.

Immersion in seawater below $-1°C$ (seawater freezes at $-1·9°C$) can cause freezing injury if the part is uncovered, so that head, hands and feet should be clothed if possible to provide the slight rise in the next-the-skin temperature necessary to avoid freezing in icy conditions.

In flooded rafts, or holed boats supported by buoyancy tanks, a close watch has to be kept on exhausted castaways while at rest, for they may inadvertently slip into unconscious-ness and drown in the water in the bottom of the survival craft. If it is not possible to keep the craft bailed, keep a separate watch on sleeping survivors to ensure that they maintain a safe posture, particularly during heavy weather or in cold conditions when the onset of hypothermic confusion may make them more vulnerable.

(6) Tropical Immersion

A type of immersion injury which has no connection with cold may be experienced by survivors who are forced to have parts of their bodies soaked in seawater for long periods. Swelling and tenderness on the tips of fingers and toes are particularly painful but this can be alleviated by making deter-mined efforts to keep the affected parts from remaining saturated. Apply a barrier cream or oil if available, although this will quickly be rubbed off the skin if it is exposed, as in tropical conditions.

Other types of skin eruptions result from long periods of seawater immersion in the form of a rash and boils, appearing first, usually, on areas of most frequent contact, ie hands, elbows, buttocks and knees and then spreading gradually to other parts of the body. Once incurred, the sores take quite a long time to heal and the pain from them is considerable and often demoralising. Try to avoid wearing wet clothing on the area of sores and if rain showers permit, wash the salt from the affected parts. Although healing takes a long time, the inflammation and pain (except through direct contact) are quickly alleviated if a 48-hour period of salt-free exposure can be achieved. Much care is necessary to avoid the onset of seawater boils and this is often not possible if survival obligations intervene. If so, a determination to endure, and an infinite sympathy for your fellows in avoiding inflicting pain when moving around, can help to compensate for and assist suffering. Established boils should be left strictly alone; any attempt to squeeze the pus from them should be resisted strongly as this results in further damage to tissue and prolongs the healing period.

(7) Other Miscellaneous Dangers

Shark attack can vary a great deal in the determination with which it is pressed home, depending on the type of shark and the condition of the survivor. It is always to the survivor's advantage to adopt an attitude of quiet aggression as most sharks will test the survivor's vulnerability by approaching closely and 'bumping' (ie hitting with nose, body or tail) before actually attacking. If a shark is struck (with the feet or fist if no wreckage is to hand), it will retreat to a safe distance and wait or find an easier prey. It is useless and dangerous to try to swim hurriedly away from a shark, for its speed through the water is far in excess of anything a swimmer can achieve. Progress should be made quietly and warily, stopping to strike if the shark approaches closely again. If the survivor is bleeding, the wound should be covered and the bleeding stopped; the survivor should then try to leave the immediate area where the blood was released as predators tend to strike at any form of life in that area, but this should be done quietly and watchfully, as already described.

Jellyfish, especially of the Portuguese man-of-war type, can cause very painful and crippling stings if inadvertently swum into, another good reason for moving carefully through the water.

Barracuda may attack live survivors although they, and other forms of scavenger fish, will strike much more boldly if their first advances to a weakening swimmer are not forcefully repulsed. Generally, the rule governing survival against attack is that those who prove able to defend themselves will be left alone, except in an attack by extremely large predators, against which normal weapons would be useless anyway.

This is a primary law of savage survival, which holds good for all time.

Cramp, although painful, is not a common cause of drowning, for this is usually associated with tired muscles. Swimmers who suffer from cramp can usefully allow the affected parts to remain idle, for this is also the way to resist the speedy onset of hypothermia. Cramp does not prevent a swimmer from floating on the surface of the water in the normal 'at rest' posture.

6 ASSESSMENT OF COURSE OF ACTION

One of the most difficult decisions has to be taken once the initial work of reviving casualties and collecting useful debris has been completed: whether to stay in the area of the sunken parent craft (as much as is allowed by wind and current) and hope for rescue; or whether to strike out immediately for the likeliest landfall.

The decision is made easier by a careful assessment of probabilities. Waiting time limits can be variously estimated if there is the probability of a search and rescue party being launched towards the scene of the disaster. Thus:

(a) If radio contact has been made through distress channels, and your plight acknowledged, try to stay as near the scene of disaster as possible. Allowances will be made by rescuers for your likely drift.

(b) If radio distress signals have been sent, at the correct time on the international wave-lengths, even if no acknowledgement has been received, a certain amount of time must be allowed for response before leaving the disaster area. This length of time can only be assessed in relation to the accuracy of the disaster position being known to the rescuers and the likelihood of a search being launched. If no search aircraft or ships are sighted within three days, alternative action should be put into effect.

(c) If portable radio beacons are carried it should be remembered that they have a very limited range (about 25 miles at sea level) but may be received by aircraft at longer distances. As in section (b), if no response is observed within three days alternative action should be taken.

(d) If no radio signal has been made, the probability of search and rescue will diminish in proportion to the size of the disaster, its commercial significance and the distance from search and rescue services. Aircraft are tracked fairly accurately and a successful search is possible if the disaster has occurred along the established route. Larger vessels are similarly well reported and investigated but smaller fishing boats and yachts cannot expect assistance until well overdue at their destination and often not then. In such cases there is little point in remaining at the site of the disaster any longer than is necessary to recover useful debris and survivors. The decision now has to be made as to the direction in which to travel. There are four major considerations to take into account, and I place these in order of importance to survival: (1) water; (2) ease of progress; (3) landfall; (4) rescue.

(1) Water

If the disaster has taken place in an area where there is little rain it is essential that the survival craft should be directed with all possible speed to the nearest area of rainfall. Consultation of the survival chart (appropriate to the time of year) in conjunction with ocean winds and currents is vital for this decision. *A wrong decision in this matter could be fatal.*

(2) Ease of Progress

This can certainly be associated with, primarily, favourable currents and/or favourable winds. Once again consultation with the chart is essential before a decision is made. In terms of effort, a survival craft can travel down wind at 40 miles a day while the occupants rest and conserve their strength. The same occupants can exhaust their lives from their bodies in an attempt to travel up wind and current without gaining a yard. Thus survivors could successfully make a landfall 2000 miles to leeward, or die in the attempt to make land 200 miles to windward against the set òf current. The decision to turn away from the nearest, but unfavourably situated, land is a very difficult one to make in survival conditions but it is often the right one.

The problem of direction having been settled, the whole concept of survival takes on different values. There is no greater morale booster than a positive course of action which can be seen to be working to the castaway's advantage.

(3) Landfall

The ultimate aim of the castaway, who should bear in mind that the land aimed for must be able to support life (and therefore probably be inhabited) and that it must be large enough to allow for errors in navigation commensurate with distance run. To travel 200 miles and hope to sight a low-lying island a mile in diameter would be stretching dead reckoning beyond the bounds of credulity. The actual sighting of the island after such a run in a survival craft would be a matter of good luck rather than good judgment. The landfall aimed for should be the largest chunk of land in the general direction of travel and survival time estimates for stores should be based on the distance of this land from the scene of the disaster.

(4) Rescue

Rescue comes regrettably last in the prospects for the castaway, not so much because the chances of sighting a ship are so remote, but rather because the chances of sighting a ship which will pass close enough to see or hear the signals of the survivors are a matter of coincidence rather than design. A raft may lie in a busy shipping lane for many days and be passed by several ships without being sighted. Or survivors may meet a solitary ship in mid-ocean and be picked up. This is particularly so since the advent of auto-pilot and radar and the castaway should be careful not to exhaust his store of flares in frustrated anguish at a ship's passing.

7 CARE OF SURVIVAL CRAFT

(1) Inflatable

Modern inflatable survival craft of approved makes are constructed from proofed fabric of sufficient strength and durability to satisfy the high standards laid down by the Safety of Life at Sea Convention (1960).

It does happen, however, that because of damage incurred during the disaster (to which inflatables are particularly vulnerable) and subsequent leakage, or because of changes in temperature, that pressure is lost from the flotation chambers. Pressure should be replaced frequently to keep the chambers rigid and so prevent the fabric from flexing in the seaway; flexing accelerates the rate of wear and, while the fabric is designed to withstand a minimum of 30 days' exposure in all sea conditions, the craft may have to last considerably longer. Care taken to preserve the fabric in the initial stages of the ordeal will therefore have a pertinent bearing on this. Any damage to the fabric should be made good as soon as possible. Usually external damage can be more easily repaired with the use of plugs than by trying to apply adhesive solution to wet fabric. Internal damage is more readily repaired with patches. Spars or paddles should not be used to support canopies on inflatable craft unless special provision is made by way of reinforcement and protection to avoid chafing by both the spars and their lashings. *Continuous chafing of this nature can destroy the fabric in a week.* Extreme care should be taken to ensure that grab lines, trip lines, towing appliances, sea anchor ropes, etc. do not foul and chafe the fabric; frequent inspections are necessary to ensure that the fabric remains chafe-free; prevention is the best repair.

The consequences of overlooking an area of chafe can result in long periods at the bellows to keep flotation chambers efficient. Often the bellows themselves are inefficient both in volume and construction. When this happens the castaways must then cut off the bellows tube and blow through it by mouth. This is an exhausting routine but it may be the only way to keep the fabric rigid until the site of the pressure loss is located and repaired. Bellows tubes should be fitted with a small junction piece near the bellows chamber to allow for this emergency procedure.

Precautions must be taken in areas of ice to protect the fabric from sharp floe edges; small granules of slush ice may also wear the fabric quickly and any form of protection which can be afforded to the fabric is better than none.

Where there are a number of occupants in a raft, care should be taken to avoid excessive wear in the positions of greatest usage, particularly around doors where watch-keeping is carried out, and on central divisions where heavy strain is imposed by occupants attempting to stretch out. The area where the floor of the raft joins the side flotation pieces is also subject to heavy stress, and although wear here may not result in loss of air pressure, it does allow a flow of seawater on to the floor of the raft; severe discomfort, salt-water boils, and probably some form of immersion injury will follow, particularly in cold-water areas.

In areas where there is much evidence of surface marine life and particularly where sharks or turtles are numerous, the fabric of the inflatable is under stress from bites and from contact with the harsh skins of these creatures; they should be warded off at every opportunity with paddles or improvised spears unless they are required for food. In rafts with canopies, in warm weather areas, holes can be made in the side of the canopy through which the occupants can strike at fish or turtles rubbing on the sides of the flotation chambers.

If game fish and sharks strike frequently at the edges of the raft, as they will in areas where there is a high dorado (or dolphin-fish) population, they may be diverted by trailing a 'skirt' of any sort of material around the edges of the raft to create an area of shadow beyond the flotation chambers (see diagram, p. 29).

When repairing worn areas the weakness of the surrounding fabric should be taken into consideration, and if repair solution or patches are in short supply, then it may be more effective to use a plug, round which the weak fabric may be gathered and then bound airtight, saving the patches for the smaller holes which will appear later (see diagram, p. 30).

When propelling inflatables by oars or paddles over long periods, take extreme care to ensure that the points of contact between fabric and oar are well protected from wear and that too much strain is not put on the fabric by an excess of zeal, especially in dual-purpose inflatables where carrying handles are used as rowlocks. It is therefore better practice to lie to the sea anchor in adverse winds than to attempt to row against them.

(2) Rigid Craft

Whereas the delicacy of inflatable fabric is fairly obvious to castaways, it is not so readily understood that in rigid craft the seams of wooden and metal boats are vulnerable to shock; fibreglass and plastic may split or shatter under severe impact; and the danger of capsize or swamping is much increased if manned by inexperienced seamen, especially in high seas. Heavy debris should be carefully warded off and heavy bumping by large sharks is readily discouraged by striking at them with oar or paddle on their close approach. Turtles are best discouraged by grasping their hind flippers and holding them captive for long enough (half a minute should be enough) to make them realise that the survival craft is not the mate they were seeking. Striking them on the head or shell takes longer and needs more energy but this

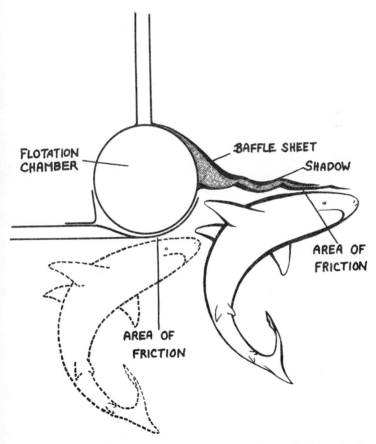

FLOTATION CHAMBER

BAFFLE SHEET

SHADOW

AREA OF FRICTION

AREA OF FRICTION

Attacks on flotation chambers may be reduced by a baffle sheet to extend area of shadow

may be the only way to deter the really big ones from bumping.

Excessive strain through attempting to beat against a short steep sea, especially with a jury rig, can cause extensive damage to small craft, to say nothing of the extreme discomfort to their crews. It is wiser to lose 20 miles in leeway than to damage the craft by trying to maintain position in adverse weather, and consequently be unable to make further progress.

Rigid craft are more stable if the occupants sit in the bottom of the boat rather than on the thwarts. Buoyancy tanks and spaces should be filled with impervious buoyant material and the risk of capsize is reduced if such buoyancy areas are close to the gunwales and away from the bottom of the boat. (This also makes it easier to right the craft if it does capsize.) A conscious awareness of the elementary principles of stability should be taught to survivors who are unused to boats at the earliest opportunity, so that they can assess the effect of their own movements on the safety of the boat. Simple practical demonstrations of how movement affects both stability and trim in favourable sea conditions can avert the need for unpleasant preventive action in times of danger.

A plug is the most effective way of stopping leaks on the outside of a raft

Rigid craft have the advantage of being more easily pro-pelled through the water by oars or paddles in calm or adverse weather but where a cutaway stern has to be presented to an unfavourable following sea, serious consideration should be given to proceeding stern first, with the bow presented to the oncoming waves; some form of drogue or sea anchor streamed from the bow is essential to allow the craft to ride easily without yawing.

Rigid craft are much less comfortable, and if no canopy is fitted, provide less protection against cold. Spars may be used to rig awnings in tropical zones, or canopies in cold weather and if few materials are to hand, efficient windbreaks can make life more tolerable than in a strictly open boat. Pressure sores on buttocks or limbs are more likely in rigid craft, especially if there is very little room to move around, and survivors should take every opportunity of changing position within the compass of the space allowed to them to prevent such sores developing.

Survival craft of all types should be kept as dry as possible to prevent the onset of skin eruptions from continuous wetting by seawater. If it is possible to prevent seawater from entering the craft by rigging canopies or effecting repairs, this should be done in preference to bailing, which is exhaust-ing and unproductive work. The amount of care taken in handling the craft can be a major factor in the length of time it remains serviceable, and it is as well to recognise this fact from the outset, rather than suffer damage from stress and strain which might have been mitigated by reefing sail or by a judicious use of the sea anchor.

8 METHODS OF PROGRESS

(1) Inflatable Craft
In inflatable craft fitted with solid keelsons, mast and sail

may be jury rigged with less fear of chafing than in other types. Only favourable winds should be used for sailing as any attempt to beat against the wind will be nullified by excessive leeway. If adverse winds are slight, paddles may be used but, otherwise, the sea anchor should be streamed until a change of wind allows further progress. In warm climates where the standard type of inflatable survival craft is fitted with a permanent canopy, better progress can be achieved by turning the open canopy door towards the wind (provided seas are not too rough) and maintaining this position by streaming a half-tripped sea anchor made fast to the towing fixtures at the doorway. If in stronger winds the sea slops into the raft the door may be closed, or turned to the lee side of the raft by transferring the sea anchor fastening to the opposite side of the raft. Progress of up to 35 miles a day can be achieved in this way. In adverse winds leeway should be restricted as much as possible by a fully opened sea anchor but in heavy seas, too much drag results in heavy buffeting and severe jerking on the raft fixtures, resulting in damage to the fabric. *This should be avoided at all costs,* either by lengthening the sea anchor lines, or fastening a weight between sea anchor and raft to act as a tension buffer (see diagram, p. 33). If oil has been collected from sun-dried bird or turtle fat, this can be used to smooth breaking seas. This is best done by placing the fat, or oil-impregnated rope fibre, in a cloth bag and streaming it on the windward side of the craft. Oil will spread to windward as the craft makes leeway.

(2) Rigid Craft

Only boats with keels may successfully beat to windward in ocean conditions where adverse seas add to leeway in reducing windward progress. Persevering in this method of progress in shallow-draft boats only exhausts the occupants, as well as subjecting the boat to undue strain and possible damage. In survival conditions it is good seamanship to sacrifice 30° of direction for the added comfort and reduced stress which this achieves. It is also good seamanship to lower the sail and ride to the sea anchor rather than risk swamping in heavy seas. The boat may be steered by an oar in place of a rudder or, if proceeding stern first with the sea anchor half tripped, by pulling down on the square sail edge on the side of the desired direction of travel (see diagram, p. 35).

In calm weather, good progress may be made by rowing, especially in an area of fairly frequent rainfall. A good water supply is essential to this form of continued progress and to exhaust survivors unnecessarily when no reasonable objective is within reach is bad seamanship and bad husbandry. In tropical zones, it is better to row at night and for the oarsmen to rest during the heat of the day.

9 STORES

When planning the distribution of survival rations the longest period of deprivation should be anticipated. Survival rations

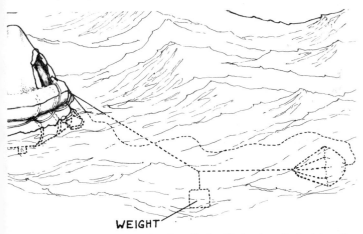

WEIGHT

A tension buffer on a sea anchor line; it should also be attached to a line joining rafts

are not maintenance rations, which recognise the body's needs over long periods of time. Until rations can be supplemented by the survivor's own efforts, or by local conditions, the initial survival ration should be the minimum which the body requires for coherent function. This allowance will vary with climate and the individual, and the following are only general guidelines established by survivors in the first two weeks after being castaway.

(1) Fresh Water

BOARD OF TRADE

MERCHANT SHIPPING NOTICE No. M.500

DRINKING OF SEA WATER BY CASTAWAYS

Seafarers are reminded that if castaway they should **NEVER UNDER ANY CIRCUMSTANCES DRINK SEA WATER** which has not been through a distillation plant, or de-salinated by chemical means.

A belief has arisen recently that it is possible to replace or supplement fresh water rations by drinking sea water in small amounts. This belief is wrong and **DANGEROUS**. Drinking untreated sea water does a thirsty man no good at all. It will lead to increased dehydration and thirst and may kill him.

Even if there is no fresh water at all it should be remembered that men have lived for many days with nothing to drink, and therefore the temptation to drink untreated sea water must be strongly resisted.

MC 54/09

Board of Trade
Marine Division, London
November 1965　　　　　　　　　**Reprinted March 1968**

In tropical areas with shade, after an initial period of 24 hours without water in order to bring the body to a low level of hydration, coherent action can be maintained for a week on as little as one third of a pint of water per day. Much more water than this is required to maintain life and after seven days, dehydration may begin to impair judgment. More substantial amounts of fluid are then required and must be obtained from other sources if rainwater is not available (see p. 39). Although the initial effects of dehydration cause much

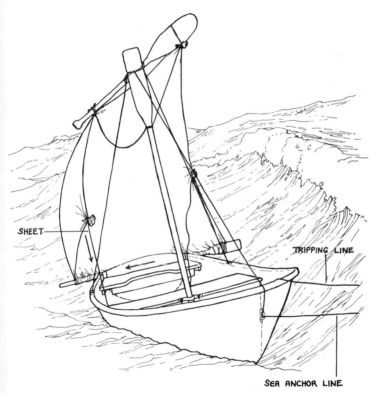

SHEET

TRIPPING LINE

SEA ANCHOR LINE

A jury rig for a yacht tender proceeding stern first. Tension of the sheet indicated pulls the stern away from a breaking crest

discomfort (foul taste, absence of saliva, weakness of legs, cracking of lips) it does not incapacitate the sufferer, but if delirium becomes established in any of the survivors, the water ration should be increased if possible to prevent the others being affected, since coherent action then becomes difficult.

If circumstances allow, the voluntary rationing of water as a self-imposed discipline is much more effective in conserving water supplies than compulsory rationing. It is, of course, essential that all the survivors join in the spirit of self-denial and do so by visual means, such as drinking from a transparent jar, but the feeling of need for water, and the desire to drink, is much lessened by the principle of self-rationing. It should not be regarded as a heinous crime if one castaway takes more than his due, but if he does so consistently, then he should be issued a ration to ensure equality.

When rain showers of short duration pass over, it often happens that water of varying salt content is collected from the catchment area, because of the need for an initial washing off period. The less salty water should be kept in reserve to use in place of good fresh water when this is needed for cleaning fabric around leaks before solution is applied, for moistening lips or any such auxiliary needs.

Foul water which is not poisonous but may cause vomiting can be absorbed rectally by means of a water retention enema. In rain storms, when all containers have been filled, additional water may also be taken in this way not only in order speedily to relieve dehydration but also as an additional method of conserving surplus water, for when the stomach shrinks in survival conditions, it is unable to hold much water. Up to a pint of water may be taken and absorbed through the rectal membrane, but it must be remembered that salt water taken in this way is equally as dangerous as if taken by mouth.

Rain should be caught and collected by means of an impervious sheet (for example, plastic) to reduce any washing off period to a minimum (see also, p. 38). Rubberised fabrics taint water, but although unpalatable, it is drinkable. Extreme care should be taken, especially in crowded rafts, to put full containers where they will not spill or suffer damage; careless handling of containers is a common cause of wastage. When opening tins of water, a very small hole should be pierced on each side of one end of the tin and the water decanted into a clear drinking jar with a lid. When the tins are to be refilled from rain, one of the holes should be enlarged so that the tin may be filled without waste. Plugs should be made ready to use immediately the can is full.

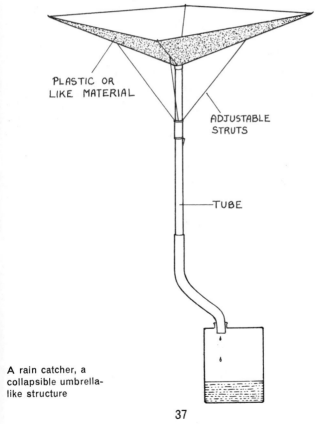

PLASTIC OR
LIKE MATERIAL

ADJUSTABLE
STRUTS

TUBE

A rain catcher, a
collapsible umbrella-
like structure

When using these refills, freshly collected water should be set aside for use in rotation after that previously collected, for it sometimes happens that taint develops (from many sources) in rainwater which is stored over long periods. In storing tins with plugs which do not fit exactly, when the plugged end is uppermost, the tops of the tins must be protected, preferably by a snap plastic top, against the intrusion of seawater from spray. It is often these small, relatively simple points of care and maintenance which are overlooked by survivors under stress and which if neglected cause loss of vital food supplies.

Condensation can sometimes be collected from surfaces which are salt-free. An example of this form of water collection is a solar still, which can give up to two pints of water a day—survival ration for six people—to span the gap until rain is collected. Makeshift condensation units can be rigged with useful results if the right materials are available and conditions are suitable, as they sometimes are in areas of water shortage (see diagram, below). Care has to be taken to avoid upsetting makeshift equipment and this can be a major factor limiting the use of stills in a rough sea.

It helps to conserve body fluids in tropical zones if clothes are soaked in sea water frequently to keep body temperatures

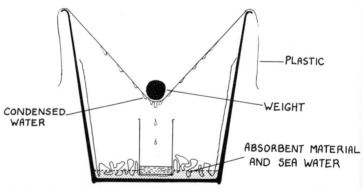

CONDENSED WATER

PLASTIC

WEIGHT

ABSORBENT MATERIAL AND SEA WATER

An improvised solar still for calm weather

down by surface evaporation. Bathing in these zones, apart from wasting energy, is not usually possible owing to the presence of sharks, particularly if fish are being caught and their offal discarded. However, much relief can be obtained by simply pouring water over yourself or your companions and bailing the surplus overboard.

In ice regions, old sea ice is salt-free. Icebergs contain fresh water ice, but the current year's ice is contaminated by salt and should not be used. Old sea ice is recognised by its smoothness and clarity, and the way it splinters easily. New ice, by comparison, is opaque, tough, and angular. Ice should be melted before tasting it for salinity, as cold tends to numb the palate.

Note. It is agreed by all competent authorities, including people who have experimented with drinking sea water in small quantities, that the drinking of sea water by anyone who is suffering some degree of dehydration will only result in increased dehydration, followed by deterioration into delirium and death. It is not possible to prevent dehydration by drinking sea water and early drinking of sea water before dehydration sets in merely reduces moral resistance to reject it when faculties are impaired.

Food in any dehydrated form need not be eaten (it will not be wanted) when water is very short, but the fluid in marine life should be taken immediately it is caught so that the full benefit of the moisture it contains may be gained. Surplus marine food should be dried and saved to eat when more water is available. Vivid dreams of fresh fruit and such delicacies are not to be mistaken for hallucinations or delirium, but are a natural reaction to the need for moisture. Delirium sometimes requires the need for physical restraint to prevent injury to the sufferer or to others.

(2) Supplementary Water Supplies

Tropical areas, where maximum dehydration conditions

exist, are fortunately populated by a large variety of marine life which, if caught and killed in the correct way, can be used to sustain the life of the castaway for long periods.

Apart from fish, the turtle is one of the most useful marine creatures which the castaway may encounter. Some species are fairly easy to catch, for they often bump the survival craft (looking for a mate) and may be hauled aboard by the hind flippers taking care to guard its beak and lacerating claws from damaging castaways or craft. Although it is difficult to kill and cut up this armoured reptile without the proper equipment, a good enough job can be done with a sharp pointed knife and perseverance. The turtle should be laid on its back, beak and claws held, and the point of the knife inserted into the neck to cut the arteries and veins close to each side of the vertebrae. The spurting blood vessel may be directed into a receptacle and three or four pints can be expected from a 75 lb turtle; the blood is not salt to taste, and is best drunk immediately while warm, as it coagulates on cooling (in about a minute) and is then difficult to drink. If the castaways are very weak, or the turtles particularly large and unmanageable, it may be found more convenient to secure the turtle alongside and drown it, rather than bring it aboard the survival craft to kill it; but if this method is used, the blood will not be so readily available for drinking, and the meat will have a much poorer keeping quality through not being bled properly. The cooler blood will very quickly coagulate but if it is distasteful to the castaway to eat this jelly, it can be cut up to release the serum which can then be drained off for drinking. The meat from the turtle which is not to be eaten immediately should be kept in a waterproof bag for an hour or so; the juice which drains from the meat can then be collected and mixed with turtle egg yolks to make a delicious sauce in which pieces of dried meat and fish can be dipped.

Fresh-tasting fluid can be obtained from the cavities in the backbones of fish, and may be sucked out after the vertebrae have been separated (see diagram, p. 41). The vertebrae of sharks, however, contain no fluid. Some species of fish have large eyes which may be sucked to obtain the fluid they contain.

The flesh of fish and turtles, as well as that of barnacles and similar shellfish which cling to ropes trailed in the sea, contains a large percentage of fresh fluid and small quantities may be eaten immediately. They may also be eaten at varying stages of drying but extra water must be taken to compensate for this. All unknown food should be taken with caution at first, to see that it does not contain harmful substances like, for instance, the stings of jellyfish in plankton.

While it is obviously not possible to lay down conditions in which the fluid contained in marine life may be consumed, in times of acute water shortage it should be assumed that if the taste is bland and unsalty, try it; if it tastes bitter or salty, reject it.

(3) Food

Many responsible authorities state that protein food should not be eaten on any day when less than two pints of water are also available. This advice may be based on the fact that an intake of two pints of water is needed to supply the body's demands for the necessary gastric juices and for the ultimate disposal of the waste products of protein matter. But it must be recognised that there is a considerable difference in the amount of water which needs to be taken

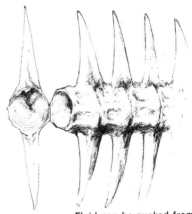

Fluid can be sucked from the spinal cavities of fish

with wet protein, such as freshly caught fish or turtle, and the same protein after it has been dried. It is also possible for the body to tolerate a build-up of waste over a period of several days, to be disposed of later by a flush of water when rain becomes available. Over long periods of survival-level living, the castaway needs to adjust his intake of food from marine life to cope with his long-term needs and to prevent his body tissue from wasting away through starvation. It has been suggested that whereas a man may live only 10 days without water, he may live 30 days without food; but during the latter stages of both periods the castaway will certainly be disabled to the extent of being incapable of self-help or of attracting the attention of a rescue vessel.

It is a first principle of survival that the castaway should try to remain coherent and able, and to this end many practical examples may be cited of castaways who, over long periods, have consumed marine food with considerably less water than two pints a day, and have remained healthy and able with no subsequent ill effects. Indeed had this rule been rigidly observed, the same castaways would undoubtedly have become severely disabled by starvation with a different conclusion to their ordeal.

It should be remembered that while caution is praiseworthy in matters of choice, the hunting savage, which the castaway has now become, has little opportunity to pick and choose in the selection or rejection of food. He may be able to reduce or increase his intake of food as available water allows, using his dried stores when water is plentiful and restricting himself to small quantities of wet, fresh food when it is scarce but such is the plight of the castaway that caution cannot be practised to the exclusion of survival demands. The adjustment to primitive eating practice should be made before desperation robs the castaway of basic good judgment of the difference between what is harmful and what is simply disagreeable. It is better to live dangerously than to die cautiously.

The flesh of most types of *marine life* may be sun-dried and stored against the time when rain will provide the castaway with enough water to use it. If there is the prospect of a relatively dry period of three days, the fish, turtle flesh, etc. may be cut into strips an inch thick and hung in the open air to dry. For quicker drying, the flesh may be shredded into much smaller strips and either laid on thwarts or canopies and turned frequently, or hung in rows fastened to lengths of small line. More fluid is leached from the flesh in this way but the drying period is reduced by half. The food may be eaten at any stage during drying, water permitting, so it is better to start the drying process immediately for marine food quickly goes bad if kept damp in hot weather.

Generally speaking, ocean and offshore fish make good eating, scavengers or not, but the offal and flesh of scavengers should be discarded if the castaway has any misgivings that the fish may be poisonous or may have fed in polluted waters. Fish livers, hearts and roes, taken in small quantities make tasty variations to diet. Large quantities of fish and turtle liver should be avoided to prevent too high an intake of liver oil which can cause illness. The liver may be pulped, and the oil strained off and used for other purposes. Several inshore varieties of fish have stings, or are poisonous to eat, and may be distinguished by their spiny appearance, their puff-up defence mechanism, or coral-eating characteristics (see pp. 44–5). Some older barracuda feed on coral-eating fish and themselves become poisonous. Inshore shellfish such as lobsters, crabs, crayfish, conch, clams, mussels, cockles, etc. make good eating and are often easier to trap than fish, but they should not be eaten if from polluted areas nor should shellfish with conical shells be handled because many are venomous.

Sea birds may provide a useful addition to diet although they are difficult to catch from a canopied raft. The wide-ranging birds, such as albatross, petrels, or frigate birds (see p. 102), seldom approach close enough to be caught by hand, but

Puffer fish

44

Top: Reef trigger fish   *Bottom*: Stone fish

gulls, boobies and the like will perch on the boat, raft or some-times on the castaways themselves. It is easier and better to skin the bird (if eating it raw) than to pluck it. Useful oil may be obtained from the fat which attaches to the skin.

The fat from birds and turtles should be collected in a plastic bag and hung in the sun. Oil is secreted from the fat and forms a very useful lubricant, protects areas of tender skin and may be used to smooth breaking seas (see p. 89). Residual fat tissue may be chewed and is very sweet-tasting, especially in colder weather.

Bones of birds and turtle bones have a very tasty marrow, which is best extracted by chewing the knuckle end and then poking it out with a pointed instrument. If a castaway's teeth are strong, turtle bones can be splintered and the marrow then licked out; many a happy hour may be passed in this manner.

Sense of smell is not a very good guide to the quality of food (either wet or dry) since the castaway quickly becomes accustomed to the disagreeable odours which emanate from drying fish, turtle or bird flesh. Quality can often be deter-mined by examining the folds of the dried meat. If they are green or slimy and have a very disagreeable taste, then the slough should be scraped off and the food thoroughly re-dried. If the fibres of the flesh have disintegrated, as is likely in continuous wet weather, it should be thrown away.

If any *emergency rations* have been saved from the disaster, these should be husbanded with great care and used only when sea food is not available, or for special occasions when stress of weather or action stretch the castaways' resources to the limit. Some of the survivors may be less able to assimi-late raw food than others (although reluctance to try it should not be confused with this inability); if so, the emergency rations could be better used to supplement the diet of the weakest.

46

(1) Fish

In temperate zones or cold water areas, line fishing may be the most practical method of catching fish. The strongest tackle should always be tried first, at all depths to the full extent of the line. If bait is taken from large hooks without a successful strike, small hooks, down to the size of very small trout hooks, should be tried. The best bait for deep-sea fishing is usually a small fish, or a piece of fish with tinsel (the small fish in the vicinity of the survival craft may be caught by net or trap — see diagram, p. 52). Surface fishing by spoon, spinner, feather or straw (see diagrams, below) should be tried at varying depths and by skimming the surface at

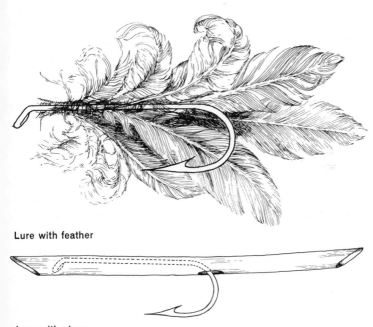

Lure with feather

Lure with straw

speed to simulate leaping fry or flying fish. Attracting fish by lure or bait is largely a matter of trial and error, but the strongest tackle should always be tried first since large fish are reluctant to return after breaking weaker tackle, but small fish become bolder if they have cleaned bait from a large hook.

When fishing is in progress, the line must always be held ready for a strike, even if it is also secured to the craft, for valuable time may be wasted if the bait is eaten from the hook unobserved, or, even worse, a small fish caught unnoticed is then taken by a large predator, resulting in the loss of valuable equipment as well as the catch. When casting away from the craft as in trolling, the end of the line should be fastened to the craft or held by a helper, otherwise the whole may be lost in a careless cast. If fastened to an inflatable raft, the line should be secured to external grab lines or at a point where it will not foul or cut the raft fabric.

In areas like the Atlantic trades, dorado or dolphin fish of average size (up to 20 lb or so) are fairly easily caught by skimming the surface with a captured flying fish, which also abound in these areas. In some tropical zones, however, particularly in areas where shark and large game fish are numerous, fishing becomes more difficult, for the hooking of one of these larger fish must result in the loss of valuable tackle. The castaways must therefore select suitable fish by other means than line fishing, and to do so they must become hunters. Infinite patience to await the right moment to strike the right fish, combined with an ability to strike instantly when that moment arrives, is an art which has to be learned by much practice and at the cost of exhausting muscular tension, but perseverance improves performance out of all recognition and the rewards are very tangible.

The two most common methods of hunting fish are by *spear* or *gaff* (see diagrams, p. 49). Spearing may be most effective if the fish is close to the surface so that force of the thrust is not absorbed by water drag. (This of course will diminish if more sophisticated spears are available.) It is better not to strike at a doubtful prey, rather than to strike without killing, for fish quickly learn to keep a respectful distance. Wounded fish also attract larger predators, which may not only be dangerous to the craft but will drive the more eligible fish away. Ground bait by day or a flashlight (if batteries are to spare) by night help to attract fish close enough to enable a strike to be made. A gaff is a safer instrument for use on an inflatable and also provides a more reliable way of securing the desired fish, especially if it is designed with hunting in mind, rather than merely as an aid to line fishing. The shaft should be 6 feet long, elliptical in shape, slender, and capable of being moved swiftly through the water horizontally as well as vertically. The hook must be very sharp and barbed and should measure 1½ inches across the curve of the shank. Both spear and gaff should be secured by a line (such as the rescue quoit line). When striking with a gaff, the barb should be inserted in the belly just behind the head so that the fish will be swimming in the direction of pull if the strike is successful (see diagram, p. 50). Game fish are powerful enough to break all but the strongest equipment if the initial thrust is misplaced and the escape dash is away from the line of pull. For this reason, an improvised gaff (see

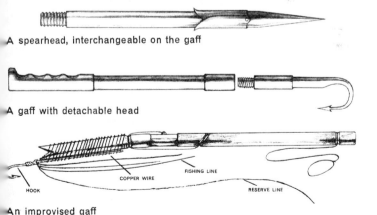

A spearhead, interchangeable on the gaff

A gaff with detachable head

HOOK   COPPER WIRE   FISHING LINE   RESERVE LINE

An improvised gaff

diagram, p. 49) must have the hook fastened so that it is rigid for striking but free to swivel immediately afterwards. If mono-filament (single strand) nylon line is used it must be checked frequently for cracks and replaced if suspect.

Improvised spears may be made by lashing a sharply pointed knife to a paddle handle but this method is risky in that a careless thrust could result in the loss of the knife, the most valuable tool in the castaway's kit, which should not be risked except as a last resort. Single scissor blades (if these are provided with the first aid kit) may be more suitable, but these should be attached to a shorter handle and used against smaller fish, tempted close to the craft by the distribution of ground bait (flying fish offal or pieces of skin, cloth, tinsel, etc.). A swift and sudden stab, followed through in an arc to propel the fish into the survival craft so that it is secured even if, in its struggles, it slides off the blade, is the most effective method of spearing small fish.

Small sharks may come close enough to survival craft (especially at night) to strike it with their tails. The alert castaway may catch such a fish by hand, for the skin is rough and gives a good grip; the tail should be secured while the fish is held and killed. Larger sharks should be beaten off with paddles or oars, especially from inflatables.

The use of nets for survival is largely restricted to the

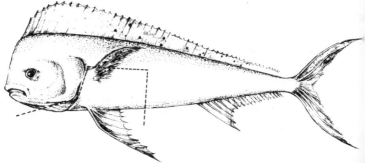

Target area for a gaff. A strike in the area enclosed by the broken line ensures the least resistance from the fish

collection of planktonic material, but the small fish which gather around to feed on offal or lie in the shade of the survival craft may also be caught by these nets (see diagram, below).

Seaweed and *grass* is mostly edible but is best collected when rainwater is available to wash out the salt. These plants contain trace elements valuable to the castaway's continued health if he is adrift for a long period of time.

If a stingray is caught, the fish should be stunned before it is brought aboard and the tail, where the sting is housed, cut off at the earliest opportunity; the 'wings' of the ray make quite good eating. Generally, fish with single spines projecting from dorsal or pectoral fins have these for protection but a painful wound can be received if they are handled carelessly.

The catching of turtles, already described on page 40, and of some types of seabird (p. 46) need not be repeated here. Birds are quickly and easily killed by placing the thumb on the back of its head and with fingers cupped under its beak give a quick backward leverage to break its neck. Some offshore birds, such as gulls, may be attracted by bait to a position in which they may be caught by hand, but others approach closely out of curiosity and this is encouraged if the castaways keep very still and quiet.

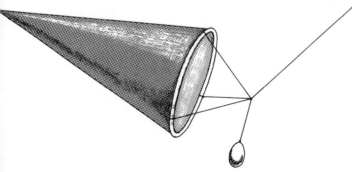

A plankton net

Many types of reef fish are poisonous, others venomous. *Poisonous fish* are usually of the coral-eating variety and have large protruding teeth or, like the parrot fish, have developed a beak suitable for grazing coral. Scavengers of reef areas may also be poisonous from feeding on the poisoned flesh of coral-eaters, and for this reason fish which puff up like balloons when caught, and reef predators, especially the older varieties, should be treated as poisonous. *Venomous reef fish* are usually distinguishable by their spiny appearance or by their veil-like appendages which can inflict very injurious stings. While these forms of fish are to be avoided (and if in doubt, don't!), there are many other forms of reef fish which are edible. An infinite variety of good eating fish, ranging from snappers, jacks, grouper, mackerel of various types, down to angel fish and large shoals of 'fry', make the rejection of the poisonous or venomous fish an easy matter to decide

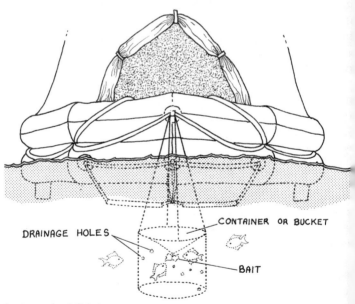

An improvised fish trap

upon in terms of food, if somewhat more difficult in terms of actual disengagement after they have been caught.

(2) How to Kill Marine Food

Most small fish in temperate zones are harmless and may be killed by a sharp blow with a stick on the back of the head or by putting a thumb in its mouth and bending the head backwards to break its neck. In tropical zones, small fish usually have a spiky projection at the dorsal fin, and sometimes on pectoral fins too, so these, and venomous fish with stings, have to be identified before being brought aboard, especially an inflatable. They should be first stunned and then made safe by cutting out stings or spikes before being brought inboard to be gutted. On inflatable rafts they should be landed on the canopy or in a thick wad of cloth while being rendered safe. Such fish should not be handled until they are safe, but should be held by gaff or spear clear of vulnerable material (including the other castaways!). Hooks should be extracted with the help of artery forceps if the fish is too dangerous to touch and the fish then thrown back.

Larger game fish may be killed by severing the head, holding them still by pressing on the eyes with thumb and middle finger, which induces a temporary paralysis in the fish. Sharks are not to be handled in this way, however, and should by held by the tail while they are killed or paralysed by stabbing it through the eye; the head is then cut off. I am told that a shark's attack may be repulsed by striking at the nerve centre on top of its head. This nerve centre behind the eyes is identified by taking the line between the eyes as the base of an equilateral triangle and striking the third angle where the sensitive area is located.

Turtles, like all animals with a copious blood supply, should be bled to death in order to improve the keeping quality of the meat. This prevents it taking on the unattractive dark colour which may be observed in bruised or badly killed meat, which goes bad quickly and is more difficult to dry in the sun. When dressing a turtle (see diagram, below), the knife should be inserted in the soft leathery skin at the head end of the belly shell and the edge of the belly shell then followed by sawing movements of the knife until the shell has been cut right around. The head end of the belly shell must then be undercut, for valuable layers of meat adhere to it as well as to the shoulder bones, the joints of which may be reached by cutting out from the centre, with the blade lying flat, close under the belly shell. The shell may then be lifted off, and the meat extracted (in four main pieces if you are experienced, in many smaller pieces if you aren't!) and the eggs harvested

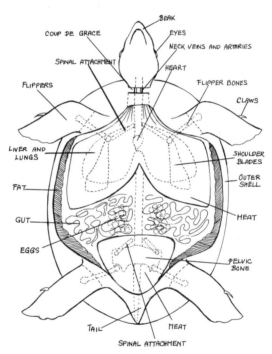

The anatomy of a female turtle (in the stag the tail protrudes beyond the shell)

if it is a female. The heart may be eaten but the offal should be discarded as suspect, especially in older turtles. The meat should then be treated as described on page 43.

Conch are best removed from their shells by breaking the pointed end of the shell where the shellfish anchors itself to the shell. A slower method is to hang the shellfish from a hook, allowing the weight of its shell to extract the fish from its protection; this is not so effective and it is better to learn to break the shell at the spot where it anchors itself.

11 NAVIGATION

Navigation in survival craft is, of necessity, the sort of rough and ready reckoning adopted by seamen before the present era of scientific calculation. The modern castaway has certain navigational knowledge at his command, however, which will help him, not only to arrive at a more accurate estimate of progress, but also to determine the direction in which he will be most likely to reach safety. The accuracy of his calculations may be of considerable importance in assessing the period of time that stores must be made to last, and his estimates should always take into account the unhappy consequences of raising false hopes in the minds of his fellow castaways. Moral stamina can be seriously undermined by a succession of disappointments over estimated times of arrival, so that it is better to err on the side of caution when you cannot confirm your progress by positive land identification.

Survival craft navigation is largely a matter of estimating the effect of the various forces of wind and current upon the craft during each twenty-four hour period and applying the set and drift to any sailing or rowing progress achieved during the period to find the day's run. A careful study of the ocean charts is necessary and, if possible, each day's run, mean course and estimated position should be noted in a log book even if no progress is made, so that the navigator should keep in close touch with the craft's position if the chart should be lost or ruined. If a compass is supplied with the emergency kit, amplitudes (bearings of rising and setting bodies) of sun and planets should be carefully recorded so that, if the compass is later lost, the recorded bearings, which only change substantially with alteration of latitude or time of year, can give subsequent guidance. The moon changes declination rapidly and is not suitable for this purpose. The compass should be checked on the Pole Star, or the Southern Cross at its zenith, at intervals to ensure that it is functioning correctly, and care must be taken to see that no metal is near enough to the compass to cause deviation when checking the course run. In order to determine this course more accurately, a small line should be streamed, its direction noted, and the reciprocal used. Magnetic variation should only be applied to a steering course if above half a point in quantity (ie 6°) since, in rough-and-ready reckoning, the finer adjustments of navigational accuracy can be

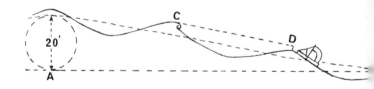

Waves

AB : Swell (caused by
distant winds)
One every 9 seconds
Height 20 feet
Length 300 feet

Swell in this case travels about three times faster than Seas ignored, for in rough-and-ready progress they cannot be implemented.

If no compass is available the course made good should be noted in relation to the direction of the primary swell and any steering carried out accordingly from this directional aid (see diagram, below). Sea swell, caused by winds from remote (as opposed to local) areas, is the one factor which is least likely to change direction without being noticed. The geographical direction of the primary (or dominant) swell should be noted at sunrise or sunset if possible, and also the direction of any cross swell which may become dominant during the period, before the opportunity to take another bearing presents itself. The wind and sea can change direction in an overcast sky without being noticed by the watchkeeper, and even in monsoon or trade wind areas, large local variations in wind direction can take place as atmospheric pressure fluctuates. The primary swell will remain constant in direction throughout these changes.

When a course is being steered, a light line should again

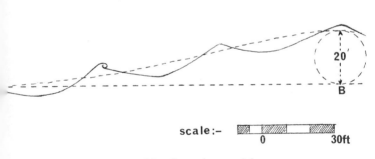

scale:– 0   30ft

CD : Seas (caused by
local winds)
One every 3-4 seconds
Height 5-10 feet
Length 50 feet

be streamed to indicate the craft's real direction of travel.

As soon as it is convenient for the navigator to do so, the position of the disaster should be determined as accurately as possible and marked on the survival charts supplied in the pocket. The first chart to be consulted when planning a route should be the chart showing drift and rainfall with ocean currents, for these will determine the only possible direction in which you will be able to travel in your survival craft. Rainwater and ease of travel are the two most vital features of the route, distance and the possibility of casual rescue being of secondary importance. It is worth repeating here that 1000 miles can be covered in 25 days, down current and wind in an inflatable raft with no paddles, while no progress at all would be made in the same craft in calm weather if paddling all the time against an unseen current. This is a hard fact to accept when habitable land lies only a hundred or so miles to windward, or up current, and the deliberate act of turning one's back on this apparent nearby salvation is one of the most difficult acts of practical survival. It is, nevertheless, the only course to take in many circumstances, for proximity to land does not, in itself, prevent death, and only an assessment of a favourable chance of rescue could justify the survivors remaining near the disaster position.

It will be immediately apparent to the castaways if the planned survival voyage will outlast their provisions and if so, they should start hunting for food without delay to establish as much as possible their independence of the emergency supplies, which should be saved for use in times of stress.

Progress need not be marked daily on the maps (which should be carefully protected from damage) but only when distinct progress is made or when it is necessary to demonstrate progress visually to the others. When further routing is necessary the position and course should then be noted on the route map, estimates made as to when shipping lanes will be approached or crossed, and more careful lookouts kept on the horizon at these periods. If entering an area of high-density shipping, serious consideration should be given to streaming the sea anchor to hold the craft in the area, but this decision will be strictly governed by the available supplies, condition of survivors, and proximity to land. *The sure successful conclusion to the voyage should always be given priority over the random chance of rescue.*

Transit from one ocean current into another may often be noted by the change in seawater temperature. The marginal areas between ocean currents of differing temperatures are often marked by distinctive up-wellings and changes in weather conditions, especially visibility, but even though the temperature change may be quite noticeable to the touch, it does not seem to make any appreciable difference to the quantity of marine life available. I have noticed that the same fish will accompany a survival raft across a temperature rise of 10°C without change of habitual behaviour.

It is not practicable to steer an inflatable survival craft directly across the wind, and this fact should be taken into account early enough in trade-wind areas so that lesser adjustments to cross wind navigation can still be made to angle the craft towards a destined landfall. Destruction of the canopy to create a sail to propel the raft is only justifiable if known habitable land is within reach by means of a jury rig which, it must be remembered, could also destroy the flotation chambers by spar or line chafing if used over longer periods of time.

Speed through the water is more easily estimated if it is related to a patch of stationary fish oil or submerged weed. Speed should not be gauged by any object protruding above the surface which is also subject to leeway. It should be remembered that the average walking pace is about three knots and it is unlikely that a wind-driven inflatable will reach this speed except in very severe weather. Normal speed in Force 5 winds will vary from one to two knots depending on the amount of drag used to keep the raft stable. It could be that the tripping of the forward stability pockets under the raft in conjunction with a half-tripped sea anchor could increase speed by a half knot while in no way detracting from the stability of the raft. Similar speeds are achieved by boats drifting to sea anchors. Careful timing of each change of wind direction over the 24-hour period is necessary to establish the distance run and mean course made good. Watchkeepers should be instructed to report these changes of wind as they occur.

Errors accumulated over a period of weeks can be quite large and it should be impressed on all survivors that, as time passes, a hundred miles' inaccuracy is a minor discrepancy over the total distance run. For this reason, it is better to err on the side of psychological advantage so that land is sighted before it is generally expected; this means establishing a dead-reckoning position astern of the estimated one.

It is very difficult to check positions with any degree of accuracy by observations of celestial bodies without instruments, especially in temperate zones. Large changes in latitude can however be detected by noting the change in the angular height of stars, low on the horizon at their zenith.

An accurate timepiece can assist the navigator to confirm longitude by the time differences in amplitudes and these signs, although vague, give support and encouragement to the survivors, who should be taught how to look for such signs in their watchkeeping routines to relieve boredom, maintain interest, and keep the final goal in mind.

Signs of bird life may also be used in loose support of the estimated position, but unless any significant phenomenon is observed, such as a seasonal migration flight, increasing bird numbers should not be taken as a sign of proximity to habitable land, especially if there are barren oceanic islands in the area. There are, however, quite distinctive patterns which, taken in conjunction with other signs, assist the navigator to establish his line of progress. The general patterns of ocean bird migration are described in Appendix B on birds and illustrated on the route chart.

12 WATCHKEEPING

Watchkeeping is an important part of the navigational routine, and if possible the same periods of the day or night should be allocated to each watchkeeper so that he is in a position to notice the changing times of amplitudes, or the altitudes of sun and stars in relation to his particular period of watchkeeping. Familiar rising and setting stars are less likely to confuse accustomed eyes into imagining a ship has been sighted, thus avoiding the subsequent upheaval and disappointment that follows such a pronouncement. Watches should be of short duration, especially if there is physical work involved, such as blowing up flotation chambers, bailing, steering, or rowing.

In bad weather, the watchkeeper needs an assistant to help in conning and bailing the raft or boat. If numbers do not permit this doubling up, then the most experienced seaman should be on call all the time and therefore be relieved of the necessity to stand watch.

Note: In rough weather when the survival craft is pitching heavily in a seaway, great care has to be taken when changing watches to ensure that water cans remain upright and that polythene containers are not in a position to be damaged by people falling on them.

In tropical waters the other principal function of the watchkeeper is to ward off the undesirable attentions of sharks or other predators, which may damage the fabric of the raft or the structure of a small boat by heavy bumping. If these bumps are frequent, two watchkeepers should be posted, one at each end of the craft, to strike the offending creature with the best weapon to hand.

Particular care to avoid eyestrain from both direct and reflected sunlight can save castaways much pain from this affliction, for which rest is the only cure. Blindness lasting several days may result from too prolonged an exposure to brilliant sunlight or to snow or ice in an icebound craft; wearing protective glasses or eyeshades in such conditions is a wise precaution.

In survival craft, watchkeepers have the added responsibility of keeping a close surveillance on exhausted companions who may move in their sleep and adopt dangerous postures which could result in their falling overboard, or, in cold weather, of checking the condition of survivors in exposed positions, who may be in danger of becoming hypothermic. Watchkeepers should familiarise themselves with the early symptoms of hypothermia and cold injury for their own protection, as well as that of others, and should not hesitate, if in doubt, to summon help. Delay in reporting a condition of this nature may result in a debilitating cold injury or an inability to keep an efficient lookout; either disablement is contrary to good survival practice however heroic or unselfish the motive. Similarly, in areas where there is a risk of severe sunburn, it is necessary to see that other survivors do not fall asleep in exposed postures, or with limbs trailing in the water where they may be attacked by bold predatory fish.

Constant attention to the condition of sea anchor ropes, knots, fishing tackle, areas of chafe, topping up pressure, bailing and sponging, drying food, and the needs of injured companions, ensure that watchkeepers on survival craft are busy people.

13 GENERAL SURVIVAL NOTES

After a prolonged period at sea in survival conditions it is natural for castaways to wonder how long their bodies will stand up to ill treatment before deterioration resulting from the many forms of deprivation will impair and finally destroy their health. Such worry is often needless, and the following information is an attempt to set out for castaways the time which needs to elapse before various bodily functions fail.

(1) Dehydration

Survival time, when no fresh water is available, varies with climate, but an estimate of ten days is considered probable in tropical conditions. When seawater is used in an attempt to sustain life, the kidneys are forced to extract extra fluid from the body to excrete the excess of salt, dehydration is accelerated and death occurs in a shorter time than if no water is taken at all.

Seasickness accelerates dehydration and exposes exhausted sufferers to the risk of hypothermia in cold weather. Injured and seasick survivors require extra rations of water to compensate for fluid losses.

Some authorities recommend that a full pint of water should be taken each day to keep survivors able; it is also stated that nothing is gained by taking a smaller ration than one pint daily since castaways who do so will quickly become enfeebled and survival time is thus shortened. However, survivors of varying bodily condition are known to have survived in a coherent and active state, in a tropical area, on as little as one-third of a pint of water per day for seven consecutive days. After a temporary respite from one heavy shower of rain, they resumed rationed supplies at the rate of half a pint per person per day for a further seven days, supplemented by an occasional intake of turtle blood. Small quantities of wet fish and turtle meat were also consumed during this period. Although a considerable amount of body condition was lost, all the survivors remained well, worked hard at watchkeeping routines of lookout duty, blowing by mouth to maintain pressure in flotation chambers, bailing, and practising hygiene.

They then went on to survive a further 23 days with

increased rainwater supplies, but often with less than one pint each per day, and, finally, after rescue they suffered no subsequent ill effects. Considerable quantities of protein in the form of fish and turtle were eaten, but during times of severe water shortage the quantities eaten were small and freshly caught. In times of plentiful rain both dried and fresh protein was eaten. Only in the first seven days were small quantities of the emergency rations (supplied in the survival craft) eaten by all the survivors. The four adults in the group then lived entirely from the sea, reserving the remaining emergency supplies for the two children. After 30 days of living entirely on raw seafood and rainwater, no physical infirmity was experienced apart from an inability to walk without support during the first day of rescue. Complete walking powers were restored 30 days after rescue and no subsequent kidney or physiological ill-effect developed.*

It would seem that there are fairly wide margins within which the castaway may take a calculated risk of disablement from renal failure due to eating raw seafood in preference to death by starvation.

Rough guidelines are that, when water intake is very low, try to restrict your diet to glucose, carbohydrates (biscuits) and fats, or to very small quantities of wet marine flesh (fresh caught, *not* dried and then reconstituted with seawater) accompanied by marine fluids such as turtle blood, spinal fluid from fish, fish eyes, or any bland-tasting (unsalty) fluid. Surplus flesh from fish and turtles should be hung up to dry; turtle fat tissues pulverised to release oil should also be hung up to dry afterwards.

When water intake increases enough to allow hunger to be felt, more wet fish may be eaten but the dried stores of fish should be saved for days when rainfall allows a fairly unrestricted ration of water. When castaways are cold from rain or other causes, increased quantities of fat or small quantities of liver oil help to maintain health and morale.

* See *Survive the Savage Sea*, Elek, 1973.

Rainwater may be absorbed through the bowel as well as by mouth to allow a more speedy recovery from dehydration, especially when a shrunken stomach does not allow much water to be drunk. A makeshift enema tube may be made from any small diameter rubber tube, such as the rubber sheathing on the ropes of the boarding ladder of rafts; this may be further tapered if a sharp knife is available. The finer end of the tube has to be inserted in the anus for about 3 inches then the outer end joined to a fairly long tube (the bellows tube will do). Water should be introduced through a funnel into the tube, held high to allow a gravity flow. Up to a pint of water can be absorbed in this way, but not too much so as to cause discomfort. The castaway so treated should lie face down, one leg bent (in a way similar to the coma position, illustrated on p. 12) and should stay in this position after the water has been introduced into the bowel for a few minutes. Only surplus fresh water which would otherwise be wasted should be used in this manner. If there is any ointment or oil to ease the entry of the tube into the anus, the patient will no doubt be suitably grateful, and 'gently' is the operative word.

When dehydration has been experienced, the volume of blood in circulation decreases, but when water again becomes plentiful, as in areas of frequent rainfall, and the volume of blood expands with rehydration, the castaway will be anaemic from this and other causes, such as imbalance of diet. Provided that varied food is available to help recovery, this condition could be helped by the taking of some form of iron supplement, which should be included in the survival kit. Anaemia causes castaways to feel lethargic and easily tired, an unwelcome addition to their troubles when rowing has to be carried out with possibly a difficult landing afterwards. In these conditions, it is unwise to continue arduous exercise, like rowing, over long periods, especially in hot weather. Frequent short spells at the oars are less harmful than allowing a castaway to become completely exhausted before resting. Exhaustion can be as demoralising as severe pain, and leaves the castaway uncaring, incapable of action in an emergency and unable to prevent the onset of hypothermia in cold weather. This is bad survival practice.

(2) Vitamin Deficiency

After a prolonged period without vitamins, particularly the 'C' group, various distinctive deficiency diseases develop. *Scurvy* is the disease which springs to mind as the great killer in sailing-ship days. In experiments conducted to encourage the onset of scurvy by deliberate deprivation of vitamins the first signs of the disease developed after 42 days, when small red haemorrhagic pustules appeared; these were followed by pains in the joints and swelling; gums became red and sore with bleeding between the teeth. It was reported from sailing ship experience that an appearance of well-being and clearmindedness developed immediately before the final collapse. Also noteworthy is that members of Scott's Antarctic expedition survived eight months without vitamin C and without developing scurvy. It has been reported that vitamin C exists in plankton, in small fish which live off plankton-eating organisms and in the green weed which grows on surface material which has been afloat for long periods. So it could be worth securing any flotsam on which this weed is growing; however it should only be eaten if surplus fresh water is available to clean off the salt. The weed can, of course, be easily kept until rain showers make this possible, simply by securing the object to which it is attached by line to the raft. Do not detach the weed until you are ready to use it.

The inclusion of multivitamin tablets in the emergency rations is therefore of some importance and in planned voyages of long duration 10 mg vitamin C per day is considered the necessary level of supply to prevent scurvy. Oranges and lemons contain twice as much vitamin C as limes, and they usually last longer too. Varying lesser quantities of vitamin C are contained in fresh fruit and vegetables. Young coconuts are a good source of vitamin C and fluid, and are much easier to open with a knife than are the older ones.

(3) Morale

As time passes, the sea and sky become familiar environs to the castaways and it is easy for them to succumb to the feeling that they may never see land again. This feeling is extremely demoralising. Every effort must be made to keep the survival craft's position, progress, and distance run to the forefront of the conscious thoughts of the survivors so that they not only remain conversant with the length of time needed to reach safety but will seek to make a positive contribution to progress. They should be informed of the reasons for regarding any setbacks as temporary, and of how they merely interrupt the sure permanent progress towards safety. For this reason, an adverse day's run should not be concealed for it will only delay the inevitable discouragement when land or shipping is not sighted at the predicted time. It should be remembered that such a setback would come at a time when morale may be lower after a longer period adrift, with a consequent loss of individual determination to carry on by those who are relying on the knowledge of others to help them.

Anxiety is a constant companion of the castaway, and is increased by feelings of fear and loneliness, especially among younger, inexperienced people. This feeling tends to make them imagine their condition to be worse than it is, both physically and in terms of their ability to endure. As time goes by in long ordeals, fears of missing a passing ship, or sailing past an island which may be just over the horizon, result in an increasing number of false reports of ships or land. Each reported sighting must be treated as initially valid until investigation proves or disproves the report, but the raising of false hopes with subsequent disappointment can be bitter blows to declining morale. It is therefore better for all concerned that an experienced person should be on call in the event of such sightings, especially at night when survivors are resting, before a general disturbance is caused with its consequent upheaval and distress, especially for any castaways suffering from seawater boils.

It is sometimes possible to hear sonic vibrations through the bottom of rafts and boats; these are mostly caused by the progress of large fish or whales, but the possibility that they come from a ship not yet sighted, or a submarine, should not be overlooked, and secondary visual distress signals, or a radio beacon, should be tried. Flares, however, should be saved until a more valid reason for firing them becomes evident.

It is as well also that an experienced person should be continuously available for consultation on such matters as craft maintenance and attack by predators, and for checking that watchkeepers are keeping an efficient lookout—with proper attention being given to sea anchor ropes, the likelihood of and readiness for rain showers, the inflation of flotation chambers—and that the craft is properly bailed out at all times to keep immersion troubles to a minimum. Sometimes instant action is necessary to avoid the loss of valuable equipment, and if a state of readiness is constantly maintained it could well mean the difference between survival and death. (For example, if a predatory shark attacks the sea anchor it can be tripped and brought close where it can be protected before it is damaged or lost.)

In rigid craft under sail, it is vital that experienced personnel should be instantly available in times of stress so that one such person, if not in charge of the steering, should be resting beside the steering position and ready for immediate action. If a castaway falls or throws himself into the sea for whatever reason, speedy action by a rescuer with a lifeline is necessary if he is to be saved before he drifts out of reach, or is attacked by predators. If the reason for the fall was mental derangement, the sufferer should be forcibly restrained in order to avoid a repetition, not only to save the life of the person involved but to demonstrate to the others that survival must be practised to the limit of endurance for everyone, and that an admission of defeat by a deranged mind should not receive sympathetic tolerance from the others. Those who decide rationally to seek death in preference to a difficult survival will have plenty of opportunity to do so inconspicuously, but the spirit of comradeship will do far more to influence such people to accept life than will the rule of authority.

All survivors should be fully aware of any damage sustained and likely to affect the safety of the craft so that they can be on constant guard against further damage or wear. Morale is seldom helped by an ignorance of the facts, but it is often badly affected by a discovery of unforeseen difficulties, or misrepresentation by those who claim to possess knowledge and are found wanting.

All the castaways should have an interest in the survival routine and be made to feel that they are a necessary part of, and are manifestly contributing to, the corporate survival. This may be simply a social function such as controlling a word game, singing, telling stories (fictional or true, they are usually received with avid interest), or instructing others in their own field of expertise. Especially popular are those who are able to conjure up word pictures of food delicacies or drinks — in fact, descriptions of anything which make easy and desirable listening. Occupational therapy can take the form of teaching the uninitiated to steer, to tie knots, to prepare and tend food for drying, or to catch and kill food where this can be encouraged without the danger of losing valuable equipment through inexpert use. Offers by keen but clumsy volunteers to use equipment which cannot be replaced and which is necessary to survival should be strongly resisted by all the others, and not left to a protest from one authoritative source.

The whole function of survival, which involves living from

the sea and creating a positive way of life upon the sea in isolation from the rest of humanity, does not include a dependence on rescue as one of the primary objectives. Rescue will come as a welcome interruption of the projected successful outcome of the survival voyage, rather than as an end in itself. While there is a strong advocacy for survival craft to be made wholly dependent on rescue, this happy conclusion for the survivors cannot always be arranged by the rescuers. In bad weather search and rescue operations fail even when full electronic co-operation is functioning, and are often abandoned when one or both communication systems cease to function effectively, as happens sometimes in times of peace and surely does so in times of international hostility. It is therefore a wise precaution, even in larger vessels, to equip a survival craft for both eventualities and thus ensure some independence of action in the event of a radio communications failure.

The most enduring factor in the personality of a castaway must be the spirit of self-denial, for if circumstances deteriorate and human beings are pushed beyond the limits of physical tolerance only their basic philosophical reserve will prevent reversion to selfish or mutually destructive practices. The basis for this philosophical reserve may lie in religious belief, or in sympathy for one's fellow sufferers, or a simple acknowledgement that this is the best way to overcome physical distress, but however the attitude is achieved, the factors which allow it to be practised must be given full scope of expression. Any authoritative instruction or direction must be confined to the realm of practical behaviour and attempts at mental domination by any one person should be resisted strongly by all the others, if only because the loss or breakdown of that one personality should not result in the abrogation of the laws of survival.

It will be difficult in this respect for those in hitherto accepted authority to avoid having this authority reinvested in them by the other survivors as a matter of course, but it is the hallmark of good survival practice that those with the required experience in any particular field of knowledge should be recognised as the authority in that field, and that pre-selected leaders, or hearsay assumptions, must be regarded with sympathetic mistrust until they are proved in practice.

It has also been significantly and increasingly established that, in human experience, there are unscrupulous people who find that, by dominating others in whatever field of human relations (by simple force of personal impact, by physical superiority, by devious educational and often deliberately false intellectual claims), they acquire the support that is necessary to keep their ego and their moral credit-worthiness at the required degree of inflation. In normal society, such people are often accepted and respected as leaders, and their errors of judgment, personal shortcomings and deceptions, concealed and even tolerated by their fellows, especially when personal gain or status is involved. In survival conditions, such people are dangerous and must be instantly exposed by those with the knowledge to do so, for simple errors of judgment, dogmatic adherence to wrong teaching or instructions, deference to protocol and other such common acts of civilised behaviour suddenly become life-or-death characteristics under conditions where a second chance is neither expected nor given. Thus the initial decisions regarding policy, direction, survival techniques, and behaviour must not be taken lightly, must not be accepted without question and must not be followed slavishly, especially if they are products of an unsound mind and will ultimately result in self-destruction. Such, for instance, would be the cause and effect of adopting cannibalism as a means of survival; of an uninformed instruction to exercise in cold water in order to keep warm; of a dogmatic adherence to written instructions even in the face of death; of a suggestion that seawater may be used for drinking, or that life itself should be the prerogative of selected individuals.

In situations where the forces of nature combine to impose

the threat of death, whether by dehydration, starvation, exhaustion or whatever cause, it will lie with the castaways themselves to decide upon the most satisfactory solution to the problem. If, for instance, water reserves have dropped to a very low level and no relief is in sight, consideration should be given to allowing the most suitable person an extra ration of water at the expense of the others so that the person so elected would remain coherent over a longer period, and so capable of action to prevent the self-destruction of the others in their subsequent delirium, or to collect rain should it come, or to fire distress rockets in the event of a vessel being sighted. While this would entail willing self-sacrifice by the majority, the self-interest of all would be the motivating force.

Similarly, when survival depends on the strength of oarsmen, then due consideration must be given, in terms of water and energy-giving food, to those who have to work so that they may serve the interests of all. Never should a suggestion of cannibalism, to alleviate starvation, be considered in a similar light, for this practice is ultimately self-destructive.

Only by a commonsense application of civilised behaviour is it possible to ensure the longest period of savage survival.

14 WEATHER FORECASTING

Although castaways have little opportunity to avoid a weather pattern, even if they know it is going to be bad, it often helps if they are able to forecast the approach of rain, or more important, recognise that certain cloud formations are unlikely to yield any rain at all and thus not be tempted to indulge in an extra ration of water at the false prospect of rain. It could also be fatal to delay an attempted landing in the face of a deteriorating weather sequence, especially if beaching is inevitable.

(1) Cloud patterns

Weather forecasting in survival conditions is largely a matter of reading cloud signs, relating them to changes of wind force and direction, and associating both with an increase or an alteration in the swell pattern (see plates, pp. 74–78).

In *temperate zones and higher latitudes,* distinctive cloud patterns herald the onset of depressions or areas of low pressure, and a typical sequence is as follows. Cirrus clouds, high, white and wispy, are followed by cirrostratus, a continuous layer of ice crystals distinguished from lower layers of cloud by the formation of a halo around sun or moon. Clouds become lower as the depression centre approaches, thickening to altostratus, a continuous, even layer of cloud which almost obscures sun or moon. As altostratus cloud thickens to obscure the sun or moon completely, rain can be expected in small amounts, evenly distributed, but not in sufficient quantities to wash the accumulated salt from the catchment area of a raft canopy or sail.

Similarly, if the survival craft is outside the central rain area of the depression, rain may not fall in sufficient quantities to collect above a pint or two, making the distribution of extra rations at this stage a move to be avoided.

If the survival craft is closer to the centre of the depression, rain will increase significantly to a continuous downpour and extra water should be immediately issued so that the maximum container space is available for refilling with freshly caught supplies. The cloud will now be low overcast with wind-driven scud, but after the passage of the warm front, the wind will change direction quite suddenly, sometimes by as much as 90°, and the weather will become warm and drizzly with a heavy overcast. Then as the cold front passes the wind will alter again quite quickly, the clouds will break and after a while, high cauliflower-like cumulus will give the chance of heavy showers which may yield more rain volume in a few minutes than has fallen in the previous hours of drizzle or light rain. Weather will then become noticeably

Top: Cirrus　　*Bottom:* Cirrostratus

74

Top: **Nimbostratus**
Bottom: **Increasing cloud at several levels**

75

Top: Stratocumulus
Bottom: Fair-weather cumulus

76

Top: Large cumulus with a shower beneath it
Bottom: Cumulonimbus

Top: Stormy sky
Bottom: Altocumulus lenticularis

colder, skies will clear with a decreasing chance of rain, some showers may die away even as they approach the survival craft, and fine weather will be re-established, sometimes with high cirrus clouds but more often with clear blue skies.

Smaller weather systems in the form of troughs of low pressure have similar cloud sequences but with smaller rain areas, although good yields may be collected. They may be identified from a survival craft by the relatively short time in which they take to develop and pass over unless they are moving only very slowly. Winds are more squally in character and sea and swell less well developed than in areas with a longer 'fetch' (distance over which they are generated). In many cases, in both established depressions and isolated troughs of low pressure, the cloud sequence will start in the established pattern as the weather system approaches but because of occlusion (when the cold front overtakes the warm), the rainfall will be much reduced, even absent, and instead of an extensive area of cloud from which rain is falling, there will be a layer of altocumulus cloud yielding little or no rain. It is not possible to tell from a survival craft whether the approaching weather system is occluded or still active, so that hopes of rain should not be raised prematurely at the sight of cirrostratus or altostratus cloud.

(2) Rainfall areas

It is difficult to predict the incidence of non-seasonal rainfall over the sea, but the principal rainfall regions of the oceans may be listed as follows. *Doldrums*: at or near the equator, rain is encountered most of the year, particularly on the side where the sun is overhead. The rain area extends over a span of about 10° of latitude and is deflected southwards in the area of the north Australian coast in December. Doldrums weather is rarely experienced south of the equator in the eastern Pacific and the Atlantic oceans, and is absent during the northern summer months in the Indian Ocean.

On each side of the Doldrums *a belt of trade winds* extends to a latitude of about 30° north and south from the equator and, except in monsoon areas (which will be dealt with separately), the weather in these regions is usually warm and dry and skies have up to 50 per cent cover with cumulus cloud in various stages of development. Occasional shallow troughs may cause showery precipitation at about ten-day intervals, but these are unreliable as a source of water to the castaway and cannot be relied upon to sustain life. Yields can be improved if proper rain-catching equipment is carried in the kit (see diagram, p. 37) instead of having to rely upon a meagre section of salt-impregnated raft canopy for catchment, but even so, if there are many survivors in the raft, supplementary water from solar stills or marine life will be required to provide a bare maintenance ration. The eastern side of the oceans have least rainfall in these latitudes, and in areas adjacent to continental deserts little or no precipitation can be expected.

In latitudes of *summer high pressure,* 30° to 40° approximately, little rainfall can be expected in the fine weather conditions which prevail in these areas, and survival conditions are difficult. In winter time as high pressure weakens and moves towards the equator the weather systems which generate in these regions can be expected to provide rain before they move into higher latitudes.

In *temperate zones* (40° to 60° latitude) fronts are experienced during most of the year and rainfall is more frequent than in the subtropical or trade-wind latitudes. Rain is less likely on the eastern sides of the oceans during spring, or during occasional summer anticyclones, but otherwise reasonable quantities of rainfall may be expected to provide a maintenance ration for castaways.

In *arctic and sub-arctic regions* frontal activity extends upwards from the temperate zones but to a much lesser degree and precipitation is not so heavy or frequent. Alternative sources of water may be available to castaways from ice in these areas.

In the *Indian Ocean* the south-west monsoon spreads northwards through the Arabian Sea and the Bay of Bengal through May to September and rainfall is heavy, particularly near the coasts of the Indian subcontinent. During the remainder of the year (October to April), the north-east monsoon brings uninterrupted dry, hot weather, especially near coasts, and survival conditions are difficult. Chances of occasional showers improve when the light north-easterly wind has crossed a few hundred miles of ocean, so that near the east coast of Ceylon, and in areas to the west and south, rain may be found in greater quantities than in north-eastern areas of the Arabian Sea and the Bay of Bengal.

Monsoon winds from the south also affect the China seas and, although much lighter, bring moisture to southern coasts of land masses from Indonesia to China; during the latter part of this period (July to October) tropical revolving storms sweep northwards up the China coast to Japan. From November to March the north-east monsoon prevails and, with strong northerly winds, brings more abundant supply of rain to areas from China to the north Australian coast. The leeward side of the large land masses have much reduced rainfalls during the appropriate monsoon periods.

In south-eastern coastal areas of the USA and the north Caribbean Sea the months of November to March bring similar blustery northerly weather accompanied by heavy rainfall at fairly frequent intervals.

Winds bring little or no rainfall when they blow continuously offshore from large continental land masses. Particular areas to note in this respect are those adjacent to the north western Australian coast, the Arabian peninsula, the Mediterranean in summer time, the west-facing coasts of Africa, the west-facing coasts of India and Burma during the north-east monsoon, and the areas to the west of California and Chile.

Tropical revolving storms occur, under various names but

with the same characteristics, in the following areas: West Atlantic and Caribbean Sea; north-east Pacific Ocean, South Pacific, north-west Pacific and China Seas; Indian Ocean, Arabian Sea, Bay of Bengal; north-western Australian coast. These storms generate around latitude 10° from the equator and are most frequent in the late summer and early autumn of the hemisphere in which they occur. They travel in a westerly direction towards the respective pole until, in a latitude of about 15°, they recurve and travel polewards in an easterly direction. On occasions, especially when continental high pressure is declining in the autumn, tropical revolving storms fail to recurve and continue to travel westwards into the mainland areas. A distinctive feature which makes the predicted path of revolving storms more reliable is the heavy ocean swell which travels outwards from the storm centre, so that the castaway has only to face the swell in order to determine the direction of the storm centre. Depending on the area in which the survival voyage is taking place, the castaways can then decide if they are in the likely path of the storm and prepare their craft accordingly for heavy weather.

Note. The information in this chapter should be used in consultation with the wind and rainfall charts, to determine whether the survival craft may be heading towards a drier or a wetter climate, so that appropriate action can be taken. In general, downwind ocean navigation will probably result in the craft travelling towards rain, for the longer the air travels over the sea, the moister it becomes with the greater likelihood of showery precipitation.

15 LANDFALL PHENOMENA

(1) Birds

When a survival craft approaches land from seaward, the first sign that land is near is usually an increase in the variety and number of birds. This is a very loose indication and should not be misinterpreted by castaways, as may be the case when crossing an overseas migration route. The route map shows the approximate location of overseas migration routes, but it must always be remembered that birds stray, become lost, or are carried out to sea in storms, and that no reliance may be placed on isolated sightings of land birds.

It is also well established that migrating land and sea birds are often influenced by seasonal winds and do not always follow the most direct route in migration flights. So, in fact, transoceanic migration routes may vary considerably from year to year and an observation of such migrating land birds is no indication of the proximity of land, or of a survival craft's position relative to a theoretical migration route.

On the other hand, it is possible to derive some hope of sighting land if seabirds which normally range within the continental shelf are sighted with increasing frequency, or if coastal migratory flights of land birds are observed. These are usually of a very distinctive nature in view of the large number of the same species of birds involved and should not be confused with a storm-driven miscellany of land birds or with a transoceanic migration of land birds. To help distinguish these ocean migrants I have tried to show on the route map the flyways used by certain species of land and shore birds as well as the areas in which the varied species of wide-ranging seabirds may be seen over the oceans.

(2) Sea and Sky Signs

As the ocean floor rises to the continental shelf the colour of the sea alters, becoming much lighter and sometimes taking a light green tinge. The extent of the continental shelves vary and approximate distances from the coast may be observed on the maps. The water may also be discoloured for many hundreds of miles out to sea by the emergence of very large rivers, as in the mouth of the Amazon, so that note must be taken of the proximity to such rivers when discoloration is noticed.

The sky reflects this discoloration and such reflection is sometimes mistaken for land loom. When land loom is visible there are usually other signs to indicate its proximity, unless it is down wind in a trade wind or monsoon area when a craft may come up with low lying land overnight; the first indication would then be the sound of breakers. Bird life and an alteration in the type of marine life may give the castaway forewarning of this. In tropical areas, the heavy scent of plant life is often carried out to sea by offshore winds and may be detected at distances of 20 miles.

In tidal waters or in areas where ocean currents run parallel to the shore, drifting branches, fruits or nuts are often seen. Sawn timber, however, may be met with anywhere in the oceans, as may an oil slick from vessels which are clearing holds or tanks. Seaweed may also be encountered frequently in mid-ocean, especially in ocean currents and in accumulation areas like the Sargasso Sea.

Lenticular cumulus often develops over a land mass or fixed cumulus cloud, which appears in a cloudless sky or amidst moving clouds, may result from vertical wind currents above an island. Large coastal cities show a loom at night which may be visible from well over 100 miles away. Lighthouses with powerful lanterns may have a loom visible at distances of 40 miles. (Some large cruise liners may also be seen from long distances but unless the actual lights themselves are visible, no attempt should be made to attract attention by hand flares, although if there are rockets to spare and the area is not much used by shipping, an attempt could be made if in good visibility.)

When land is sighted, it should be remembered that high mountains may be seen at a distance of 50 miles in clear weather and that it may take three or four days to reach such land, perhaps longer if offshore winds are experienced at night

In colder zones, atmospheric stability may cause abnormal refraction enabling sea level objects to be sighted at distances of 40 miles with considerable clarity. This is not an hallucination or mirage, and experienced seamen can recognise the weather conditions which make these sightings possible; they are usually associated with an atmospheric condition in which warm air exists above a cold surface, causing rays of light to be bent over the horizon. This may also cause objects to appear upside down or with other considerable distortions; these should not be mistaken for hallucinations either, but such conditions may not be suitable for the sighting of distress flares. Smoke or heliograph should be used until the object is well within normal sight before distress flares are used, otherwise they may be wasted.

6 LANDING ON SHORE

A considerable amount of advice has been written about landing from a survival craft in heavy surf. Only general directions can be given, for the forces involved may not allow freedom of action; but if the choice is available, *do not land in a surf.* Castaways in a condition of physical deterioration, particularly from dehydration, will be unable to walk, possibly unable to stand, and certainly unable to struggle for any length of time in the violence of a breaking surf and some will almost certainly die if such a landing is attempted.

(1) In Inflatable Craft

On approaching land in an inflatable it may be impossible to avoid being carried on to the beach by an onshore wind and selection of the best landing spot should therefore be made as early as possible so that any cross-wind navigation may be carried out. Since it is extremely difficult to gauge the extent of the surf from seaward, the nature of the beach coupled with its angle to the breaking surf, should be the basis of selection (see diagram, p. 88). If possible never drive directly on to a shore which faces seaward and lies parallel to the approaching waves since this is the area where there will be the highest incidence of rock and undertow, with the most violent breakers.

On approaching the shore, lash stores and water to the raft, if possible in watertight containers, cut the canopy away from the flotation chambers at the sides of the raft, so that escape will be more easily effected if the raft is overturned or deflated and then stay with the raft for as long as possible. Ground swell will increase and as the raft surges to the top of the swell, try to glimpse an area where a shelving beach will allow survivors to crawl above the water line. It is important to remember here that dehydrated survivors will be unable to walk. A light sea anchor at this stage will help to keep the raft from capsizing prematurely in the surf. As soon as the primary breakers are reached survivors should be congregated at the seaward side of the raft with the strong swimmers in the water holding on to the grab lines to keep the raft stable. Life jackets and clothing should be worn for protection against pounding on sharp rocks and coral. The raft should be filled with seawater before entering a heavy primary surf (by piercing the raft floor if necessary) to

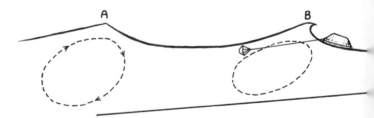

SURF DIAGRAM—PROFILE

(A) When a wave builds up on approaching land this is distinctly noticeable when the depth of water becomes less than half the wave length from crest to crest

(B) Surf begins to break when depth of water is $1\frac{1}{2}$ times the wave height help stability, but in cold water this should not be done until the latest moment to ensure the shortest spell of immersion. If the water is very cold the castaways must decide for themselves whether the cold or the surf is the greater danger, and flood the raft or not accordingly. However, a capsized raft is going to flood anyway, and it is difficult to prevent capsize if the surf is violent. If the raft is overturned, cling to the grablines but be prepared to make for the shore independently, for the raft can now cause severe injury if a survivor is trapped between it and a rocky seabed. The raft may be re-joined when the violence of the primary breakers has been passed, for if it is still afloat, it is still the best means of transporting the weaker survivors to the shore. The raft remains should be assisted ashore by the stronger survivors so that the stores and equipment lashed within can be saved before they are damaged beyond recovery. Very weak survivors should remain within the raft at all times for their chances of surviving a violent surf independently are not good.

(2) In Rigid Craft

When approaching land in a rigid craft a different technique must be adopted. If oars are available, the craft should be

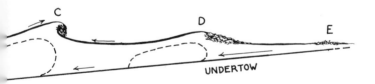

(C) Surf breaks heavily when depth equals wave height. At this point the survival craft enters the area of danger to castaways through injury from the craft itself

(C) through (D). Area of strongest undertow where weakened castaways are at maximum risk through injury from the seabed and from drowning

(D) to (E). Survivors who have reached safety should remain in this area to assist others at point (D)

held off the shore and navigated round the coast until a sheltered landing place is located, or until the help of local inhabitants can be enlisted. *No deliberate attempt should be made to land a rigid boat in a heavy surf.* It is far easier for survivors to travel round the coast by boat than on foot, and, in a raging surf, the boat which has sustained

SURF DIAGRAM—REFRACTION

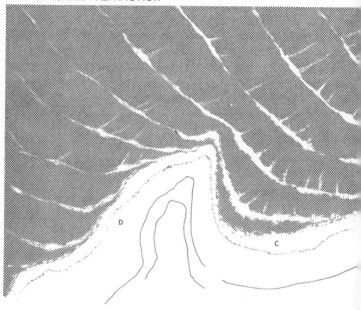

(A) 'Steep to' headland produces area of confused seas dangerous to all craft
(B) The best area for landing is on the opposite side of a 'steep to' headland and where surf makes the largest angle to the original wave direction
(C) Difficult conditions, with surf of long duration, and severe undertow
(D) Next-best landing area to (B). Surf is reduced by half when it is deflected by more than $100°$ from its original direction

life at sea becomes a fearful weapon of destruction to castaways struggling in the water.

If a landing is unavoidable because of storm conditions,
and the boat has to be beached, the sea anchor should be
streamed to present the most seaworthy part of the boat to
the oncoming waves. The oil bag, if available, should be well
filled and fixed to the sea anchor; any other oil available
should be held in water tins with slow
leakage holes ready to release before
entering the surf. As the crests of the
waves approach, the sea anchor
should be streamed full open but as
soon as the forward impetus of the
crest is experienced the sea anchor
must be immediately tripped and the
boat assisted to run in on the back of
the breaker; the sea anchor should
again be allowed to open fully as the
next crest approaches (The tripped.
sea anchor will not appreciably hinder
the boat's assisted progress towards
the shore and has great value in preventing the boat from 'broaching to'
as the crest approaches.) When and
if the boat finally overturns the sea
anchor should be left open to prevent
the boat's further speedy progress

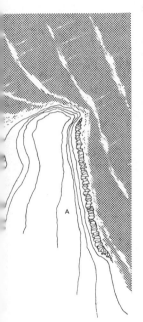

inshore where it could smash down on top of the survivors
struggling in the water.

Light flotation pieces of polystyrene or lifejackets should
be used to help survivors to ride the surf in towards the shore
ahead of the craft; avoid oars or heavy thwarts as a means of
support as these can inflict crippling blows in a heavy surf.
The boat will eventually be washed ashore and any pieces of
equipment lashed to it should be recovered at the earliest

opportunity before they are dispersed if the boat should break up.

When survivors are forced to take to the surf, some may become unconscious through cold, fatigue, near-drowning, or by the buffeting from the surf. It will fall to the conscious survivors to try to remain with and bring ashore these casualties. It is imperative that the weak and injured be removed from the water quickly before they drown, and those who have reached a position of safety should not proceed further towards the shore without looking around and helping those in need. Sharp rock or coral outcrops may lacerate buoyancy apparatus or lifejackets and valuable stores of food and water, as well as lives, may be lost at this time, so it is worth repeating that survivors with adequate reserves of strength should remain as near the surf as safety permits, to carry out rescue and salvage operations. In tropical zones, legs and feet should be covered to protect them from contact with sea urchins, especially in rocky areas; oilskins will give the body some protection against the penetration of urchin spines, which can cause very painful stings especially where pressure is unavoidable, as on the soles of the feet and palms of hands.

17 LIVING FROM THE LAND

(1) On Islands
If the condition of the survival craft makes it imperative to land on a remote island or uninhabited shore, there are ways in which life may be made more tolerable until a rescue is effected. A study of primitive tribal life in remote areas establishes the best methods in which survival may be continued for an indefinite period. The following are personal observations of existing practices.

On small low-lying coral islands with palm trees as the

principal vegetation, water holes for sweet water should be dug inside the vegetation line and not in the sand on the beach. This does not include mangrove trees which grow with their roots in salt water. A low-lying area should be selected for the water hole since the water table will be level across the island.

A wide variety of edible marine life exists within the shallow reef area from conch (which makes very fine soup) and other shellfish to a wide variety of small reef fish, which may be caught easily with the small hooks, using pieces of crushed crab for bait.

Very small fry are difficult to catch without a baited fine mesh net but a swift blow with a paddle on the seaward side of a shoal of small fry swimming close to the beach may panic some into stranding or may stun some if they are very close to the surface. They make excellent bait with which to catch jack and other such larger edible reef fish. Spear fishing in deep water reef areas is difficult without a mask but in shallow areas crayfish and lobsters may be caught, especially at night with the aid of a light. Care is necessary to avoid stepping on venomous fish or small sting rays which lie in the sand in shallow water. Small sharks may also be found in shallow reef areas and these can be readily speared or gaffed but larger varieties of shark in deeper water should always be avoided.

Larger barracuda, jack, snappers, etc. can be taken on heavier lines using small jack as bait and trolling swiftly, but the tackle can be lost in bottom fishing if a grouper or rock fish is caught and allowed to 'hole up' through inattentive fishing. Avoid eating older barracuda, parrot fish, puffer fish, or large-toothed coral eaters as their flesh is often poisonous. Fish with stings can be eaten but care is necessary to avoid injury in catching them. A precaution worth noting is that if a grouper is caught, it should be carried by the tail, or by the thumb and finger in the eyes, since the gills have needle-like teeth which can inflict painful injury if the fingers are trapped in them. Most small eels make good eating though care is necessary to avoid being bitten, but do not allow this to deter you from catching them if the opportunity offers. White crab meat, of both sea and land crabs, is edible, although a considerable number of the smaller type are required for a meal.

Shelters may be constructed from palm leaves in small clearings and where islands are in trade wind areas, these are usually built on the windward side where coolness and freedom from insects make life easier. Fires of coconut husks may be made for cooking and also for drying fish on wooden racks. Since fuel is scarce and difficult to obtain, it is important to be able to light fires easily and the magnifying glass becomes a most valuable piece of equipment.

In more temperate zones, water is not usually available on uninhabitated or rocky islands; the castaway is therefore more dependent on rain collection or distillation from sea-water if a fire and containers in which to boil water are available. Fishing is usually good and bird life plentiful, but driftwood is often the only source of fuel and the remains of the survival craft the only shelter. A certain amount of fuel should be set aside for making smoke to attract the attention of passing craft before the discharge of distress flares.

The continuation of a savage way of life may be necessary for a long period on such an island, for passing ships do not always approach near enough to detect signals. The more permanent distress signals are therefore more likely to be observed (ie 'A square flag having either above or below it, a ball') if placed in a conspicuous skyline position.

If subjected to a long period of island survival, it will be necessary to supplement a marine diet with the necessary vegetable supplements to prevent the onset of scurvy or other deficiency diseases. If the obvious vitamin sources, such as coconuts, edible fruits or vegetation are available, there will be a ready solution to the problem, but if a rocky islet with no vegetation has to be accepted as refuge, then green weed on the water line, some forms of seaweed, and green mosses may contain the necessary elements. Small quantities taken daily are more beneficial than occasional bouts of over-eating, which could result in illness.

(2) On the Mainland

If the landing takes place in a jungle or desert area far from civilisation, it is probably better to seek help by making short coastal voyages in the survival craft if the surf permits; otherwise, it is better for the weaker members of the party to establish a base at the coast while the most able survivors seek help. There is nothing to be gained by the weaker members of the party hindering a cross-country expedition in search of help. Indeed the privations of such an overland journey would be more likely to have disastrous consequences for a weakened survivor, and present the more able survivors with the unenviable duty of leaving the casualty behind in a position which may be difficult to identify later. Coastal positions are always easier to rediscover in search and rescue expeditions, and they are usually, because of the proximity of the sea, easier country in which to find a living. In the tropics, coastal areas are cooler and less populated by insect life. Any attempt to make a cross-country journey in jungle or heavy scrub without the proper equipment and a good reserve of stamina will end in death. Travellers must keep to trails or paths even if they appear to go in the wrong direction. It takes more energy to fight through half a mile of tangled jungle or scrub, even with a machete, than to walk five miles along a trail.

An important point to remember here is that if fresh water is carried by survivors who have become normally hydrated again after a spell of plenty, salt should also be carried, in the form of seawater if no other source is possible. Once away from the proximity of a salt-laden environment, a deficiency of salt can quickly incapacitate an otherwise healthy survivor. Sea salt is in common use for the supply of human needs, but only enough should be taken to maintain health. The excess of sodium chloride in seawater cannot be tolerated by human bodies unless non-saline fluids in normal quantities are also available.

APPENDIX A: SUGGESTED EQUIPMENT FOR A SURVIVAL CRAFT

(1) Water and Food

Water in tins: 5 pints per person.

Glucose sweets: 20 oz per person.

Hard biscuits: (vitamin fortified) 10 oz per person. To be reserved until water is available.

Any supplementary food should be chosen for its keeping quality, energy or vitamin content. For ease of distribution, avoid crumbly substances, which are difficult to pass around and eat on an unsteady craft. The more individually they are packed, the better, for seawater may enter an opened box and spoil valuable quantities of food.

(2) Fishing Equipment

Good quality lines of varying size from 25 lb to over 100 lb breaking strain and not less than 50 fathoms of each. (Fishing line may be required for many other purposes.) Also stainless steel trace wire, for use with larger lines, preferably with hooks already attached. It is unlikely that the speed of the survival craft will be fast enough to allow trolling (at least four knots), so lines will have to be cast and pulled in swiftly if game fish are sought. Medium lead weights of torpedo shape to fasten around the line are best for this purpose, so that the line will be carried out well when cast but will not sink too quickly. Hooks are best baited with whole small fish and pulled swiftly across the surface of the sea (sometimes fast enough to allow the bait to skip) or with other lures described in the section on page 47. Heavier weights are required if baited large hooks are to sink swiftly below the reach of surface small fry or scavenger fish. In this case it is necessary to cast well out to avoid the scavenger fish surrounding the survival craft. Hooks should range in size from very small trout hooks upwards. In certain areas, line fishing may not be practicable (p. 48) and other methods will have to be adopted. Gaff and spears are the best selective hunting weapons, and the type of gaff illustrated (p. 49) could usefully be included in the survival kit, while a Hawaiian sling or spear gun should be high priority if time allows when abandoning the parent craft. It should, however, be remembered that some strength is required to operate a Hawaiian sling, whereas the gaff is merely pulled into the fish. A spear gun with a trigger mechanism is also fairly easy to operate. Ensure that a guard is secured around any sharp points.

A fine muslin net, of the type illustrated (p. 51), may not only be used for catching plankton, but also for the storage of dried fish and turtle which tends to sweat if kept in plastic bags. Part-dried food also tends to warm up by a form of spontaneous combustion if put together before thoroughly dry, and this causes it to go mouldy. It should be frequently inspected and aired to prevent this happening in the initial stages of storage.

(3) Water Containers

One of the most important items of equipment to be stored in a kit are the spare water containers. For obvious reasons of bulk and weight, large quantities of water or desalting apparatus cannot be stored, but once heavy rain is encountered, water problems can be greatly alleviated if adequate storage is available. There is no reason why three or four gallons of container space per person should not be stowed in the kit in the form of tough durable waterproof bags which, when filled with fresh rainwater, may be floated alongside the craft or towed astern. The bags should be strong enough to use as pillows, to resist damage when fallen on, and to act as buoyancy apparatus in a heavy surf.

(4) Other Equipment for an Inflatable Craft for Ten People

Repair outfit consisting of:

    Two patches 1 foot square

    Six patches 3 inches square

    Twenty patches 1 inch square

    Repair clamp and hole stoppers (including pinhole stoppers)

    Solution (three tubes)

    Epoxy resin (two tubes)

    Leak finder

    Glass paper

One pint bailers: three (one for each end of the raft and one spare for use as urinal)

Quarter pint beakers: six (to be used as feeding cups)

One pint, clear, screw-topped jar for use as a water bottle to pass round

Mopping-up sponges: four

Sea anchors: two, with tripping lines and oil bags

Bellows: of good quality, in particular with reference to non-return valve. Bellows tube should be long enough for watchkeeper to reach all inflation valves without disturbing other people

Mouthpiece for bellows pipe in case the bellows fail

Can openers: six (of the type that makes a large triangular hole to make refilling easy)

Flashlight: suitable for signalling, waterproof, with spare batteries and bulb, with wrist-strap

Knife: one of the blunt-nosed type

Knife: one pointed blade of at least 6 inches, single-edged and sheathed

Knife sharpener: one, of the wheeled type for stainless steel blades

Electricians' or forceps-type pincers: one (particularly useful in releasing valves and making tools)

Paddles: three, sectional

Rescue quoit with 20 fathoms $\frac{1}{4}$ inch nylon line (one for each door)

Solar stills: five

Heliograph: one

Rain catcher: one (plastic material)

Plastic buckets: two (2 or 3 gallon type)

Plastic bags two foot-square: two (dry storage of goods)

Compass: one pocket type, luminous

Radio beacon: one activated by sea cell battery

Magnifying glass: two (one reading)

Handflares: six

Rocket flares: two

Smoke flares: two

In cold-water areas: A waterproof survival suit or bag may save the life of a survivor suffering from acute hypothermia and hoods and gloves may usefully be stowed for use by lookouts

One good survival book, with charts, maps, paper, pens and pencils, sheathed dividers and 6-inch rule

Sunglasses: two pairs

Supplementary equipment for rigid craft would include repair kit composed of tools (small hacksaw, epoxy resin, nails) but would still include repair patches

(5) First-Aid Equipment

Injuries incurred at the time of the disaster should be treated in the manner directed by good medical practice wherever this is possible. In survival conditions this is not easy to achieve even by practised seafarers who are also doctors, therefore medicine and equipment should be of the type which requires the least expertise in administering or use and involves the least amount of attention after application. The first-aid equipment is inevitably subject to diverse other requirements, and should be assembled with this in mind;

it doesn't help if first-aid equipment is made in such a way that it is deliberately awkward to use for other purposes, for the good survivor will always try to put it to other uses, and whether he does so successfully or not is immaterial to the first-aid box, once it has been used. When making up a kit, it should be remembered that:

Adhesive tape is more economical than bandages, and is generally a more useful material for binding objects together. Triangular bandages have many uses and should be given preference over ribbon-type dressings which are difficult to use again, once soiled.

Safety pins are very easy to lose in odd corners of a raft, where they may cause chafing damage. (It may be argued that safety pins may be used to catch fish but fish-hooks are undoubtedly more suitable.)

Tapes secure dressings more efficiently than pins, if with a little more trouble, and have many alternative applications in an inflatable raft.

Surgical needles, pre-threaded, save much time in stitching bad wounds; they can also be used to stitch bad gashes in raft fabric.

Standard, ready-to-apply dressings for wounds become sodden with seawater very quickly, as does cotton wool unless protected by a waterproof covering.

Small, shaped, inflatable cushions or splints are easily stowed and are very useful for protecting injured limbs against knocks from other castaways. They have many alternative uses. Useful splints may also be made from glass fibre and resin, which also have important repair applications.

Artery forceps should be of good-quality stainless steel and strong enough to use as pincers for other jobs around the craft. This is one of the most useful tools in the whole survival kit.

Sharply pointed forceps, for extracting splinters, can be kept in a sheath until required. They are most useful where small cavities require probing (non-return valves on bellows and raft, etc.).

Scissors should also be sharply pointed (and sheathed) so that the blades may be used as spearheads or knives if necessary.

Scalpel blades with foil sheaths are extremely useful for paring rubber, dressing turtles, and dressing fish, apart from their normal medical uses.

An enema tube would also be a useful addition with a special pint-sized enema bag to contain water.

Medicinal substances: Anti-seasickness tablets, which cause drowsiness, should not be taken by all the survivors in a raft, particularly in cold-weather areas where a major leak of carbon dioxide into an enclosed canopy would not be detected, if none of the occupants was sufficiently alert. Anti-seasickness suppositories are useful where seasickness has already started and pills cannot be swallowed.

Antiseptic barrier cream used on skin surfaces should be protected from contact with raft fabric which quickly rubs it off.

Petroleum jelly may also be used to keep metal accessories free from corrosion.

Soluble aspirin should be individually wrapped in foil, or in small quantities in airtight packets.

Eye ointment and drops may well be needed.

Antibiotics are required for treatment of sepsis and for cases of severe burn; also for lung infection which may result from near drowning or hypothermia.

Multivitamin tablets in small watertight containers to be taken daily as a protection against scurvy, etc. (These may include some form of iron supplement.)

Bicarbonate of soda in small (acceptable) quantities can assist in counteracting acidity in recovered drowning and hypothermic survivors.

Some form of *calcium,* if not included in the stores, should be supplied in the first-aid kit. Milk tablets could usefully fill this need.

Morphine injection capsules, for use when extreme pain is causing too much distress, or when violence in delirium, or from other causes, cannot be treated in any other way.

Remarks

A comb promotes good hygiene, keeping hair tidy and giving a feeling of well-being.

Skin conditions from saltwater immersion sometimes cause extensive areas of tenderness around the crutch and under arms. If in the tropics, discard wet clothing which aggravates this condition and try to keep the affected area dry. This advice need not interfere with that of keeping clothing wet during the heat of the day, for such clothing can be arranged to avoid contact with the sore area of skin. Wash in fresh water if showers permit.

Do not expect *bowel movements* when living on survival rations. These may eventually take place if adequate fresh water and seafood are available but castaways have gone thirty days without bowel movement, with no ill effects, and while eating small quantities of fish or turtle each day. Fresh-water enemas, if the water is to spare, can assist the castaway in ease of bowel movement. Urination should continue at a much reduced rate daily even while the castaway is dehydrated and although the urine becomes dark coloured and is sometimes painful to pass, this is neither unusual, nor harmful in conditions of dehydration. Urine should not be drunk.

APPENDIX B: BIRDS

Many sea birds undertake such extensive migration flights that in some cases it seems that a large part of their lives is occupied with the business of travelling to and from their seasonal habitats. Some land birds also undertake long flights overseas on regular migration routes and in the following pages the general routes which they follow, and the sea areas in which they may be encountered, are listed. There are, of course, many vagrant flights which take place under difficult weather conditions, or simply by a failure, particularly in young birds, to navigate properly. The number of birds involved in these vagrant flights is small enough to enable the castaway to distinguish quite easily between a true migration and a wayward group of birds so that an unexpected encounter with a stray flight can be recognised and noted in its proper context.

For seaborne castaways, bird life is the closest, possibly the only, link with the environment which they are striving to regain (apart from being a practical source of food in time of need) and it is hoped that this section will help towards a better understanding of the activities of the birds which are likely to be encountered on the high seas (see also plates and diagrams as a guide to identification).

(1) Oceanic Sea Birds
(a) *Albatross*

Southern oceans: *wandering, royal, waved*

North Pacific: *Laysan, black-footed*

The albatross is found mainly in the southern hemisphere; it spends most of its life over the ocean, where it depends on variations of wind velocities for flight. It lands, only to nest, on small islands and atolls once every two years, and may perform a complete circumnavigation of the world in the southern seas between nesting periods. Nesting grounds are usually on top of high cliffs on the windward side of islands to facilitate take-off.

The *Laysan* and *black-footed albatross* inhabit the northern Pacific Ocean, nesting on Laysan Island 1000 miles west of Hawaii and also on other isolated north Pacific islands such

Wandering albatross, 48″

Galapagos (waved) albatross, 28″

Black-footed albatross, 28″

as Midway, and have characteristics similar to those of the southern albatross.

(b) *Petrel*
Wilson's, Leach's, storm
Seasonal flights of various species of petrel cover enormous areas of ocean.

Storm petrel, 6″

Wilson's petrel, 7″

Leach's petrel, 8″

Giant petrel, 36″

Wilson's petrel breeds in the American sector of Antarctica during summer (January and February). They travel northwards in flocks during March and April, by which time they cover a large area of the southern Atlantic and the western North Atlantic. By June, Wilson's petrels have migrated into the northern Atlantic and may be found in large groups, sometimes 1000 strong, off the American coast and are generally distributed over the area covered by the Gulf Stream. September and October find large numbers moving to the eastern Atlantic and then southwards, following the pattern of prevailing winds to travel along the South American coast (to their breeding grounds in the Antarctic), where they remain until February. Migration does not occur along established routes but more as a general drift along belts of prevailing winds. In other areas, Wilson's petrel moves northwards from the Antarctic continent to the seas around north Australia and New Guinea, while in the Pacific it migrates along the line of the Humboldt current as far as the Doldrums. From the Indian Ocean, Wilson's petrel moves north into the Red Sea, often in large numbers.

Leach's petrel breeds in the northern hemisphere on both sides of the Atlantic: from Massachusetts northwards, in an area which includes Newfoundland and Greenland to the British Isles; and similarly in the Pacific from Canada across the islands to Japan. In the northern winter it migrates to the South Atlantic and the eastern Pacific oceans.

The *storm petrel* of the eastern North Atlantic which may also be found in the Mediterranean is smaller than Wilson's or Leach's and nests on the shores of the European continent, migrating during the northern winter to the Red Sea and the South African sea areas.

The giant petrel breeds around Antarctica and is to be found as far north as the subtropical latitudes around the whole of the southern hemisphere.

Cape petrel or *pigeon* breeds around the Antarctic islands and southern capes. It may be found as far as latitude 20° S outside the breeding season.

It will thus be seen that petrels of these and other varieties may be found in most oceanic waters of the world and their adjoining seas. They eat planktonic material and other small marine organisms, usually obtaining their food by fluttering low over the surface of the water; sometimes they maintain their balance by paddling their feet in the sea while still in flight.

Long-tailed skua, 22″

Arctic skua, 18″

Pomarine skua, 20″

Great skua, in flight showing white wing-patches, 23″

(c) *Skua* or *Jaeger*

Great skua. Usually restricted to waters in middle or high latitudes, great skuas are found in both hemispheres, sometimes crossing the equator in their wide ranging flights which are more nomadic than migratory. They are parasitic by nature and may approach closely enough to a survival craft to be caught if bait is laid out.

Arctic, long-tailed, and *Pomarine skuas (or Jaegers)* are all northern species and nest in the Arctic tundras, wintering to the south in the Atlantic and Pacific. The skua is probably the most northerly and southerly-ranging species of bird, some individual sightings having been reported quite close to the poles.

Fulmar, 18″

(d) Fulmar

Another sea bird with wide distribution is the fulmar, which breeds in middle and high northern latitudes. During the breeding season it may be found up to 600 miles from its

Short-tailed shearwater, 14″

White-faced shearwater, 16″

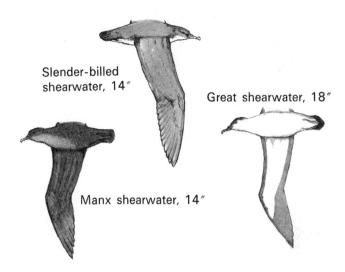

Slender-billed shearwater, 14″

Great shearwater, 18″

Manx shearwater, 14″

breeding ground and has a wide ocean distribution at other times of the year; a slightly different species of fulmar spreads northwards from its breeding grounds in Antarctica into subtropical southern ocean regions.

(e) Shearwaters
Greater, sooty, short-tailed, flesh-footed (Indian Ocean), Manx
Greater shearwaters may be found over the whole of the Atlantic Ocean from the Falkland Islands to Greenland, with migratory flights, emanating from Tristan da Cunha, in a similar pattern to those of Wilson's petrel. After their nesting period from January to March, they move north and may be found on the Grand Banks of Newfoundland in June; they then fly eastwards to Greenland and Iceland, reaching the British Isles in August. The western Atlantic birds fly southwards again from mid-August but in the east they remain around Europe until late October before moving south again.

The Pacific Ocean is also well populated by the *short-tailed* (or *slender-billed*) *shearwater*, which performs a cyclical flight from its nesting area around Tasmania and South

Australia, crossing the Tasman sea to New Zealand and moving northwards to Japan around June. It then crosses the North Pacific from west to east in the northern summer, turns south along the eastern Pacific in August, and returns to its breeding grounds by a direct route from California to Australia in September.

The Indian Ocean also has its species of shearwater, notably the *flesh* or *pale-footed shearwater* of eastern Australia, while the *Manx shearwater* breeds on the islands and coasts of the North Atlantic, migrating into the South Atlantic during the appropriate summer seasons.

Shearwaters, like petrels, have been used by fishermen as bait and may be caught in large numbers when on actual migration flights (a torch may be of help in this at night), but trapping is extremely difficult when dispersal has taken place after the destination has been reached. Shearwaters, larger than the petrels, are used for food in southern Australia, and valuable oil may be extracted from both species.

(f) Terns
Arctic, common, sooty, brown noddy, roseate, fairy

The *Arctic tern* has probably the longest migration flight of any bird. It nests along the northern coasts of Europe, Asia, and North America during the northern summer and spends the northern winter in the Antarctic having migrated through nearly 140° of latitude. Autumn flights of American and European birds move down the eastern Atlantic, avoiding the warmer western waters and, of course, following the cyclical wind pattern. Similarly, Pacific migrations take place along the west coast of the USA. The Arctic tern begins migration from the northern hemisphere at the end of July in the west, continuing into October in eastern regions. The return flight in the spring generally follows the eastern coasts of South and North America in the Atlantic but some may be found near the African Coast; they arrive in Europe in April and disperse eastwards, as do the American coastal birds, but

Arctic tern, 15″

Common tern, 15″

111

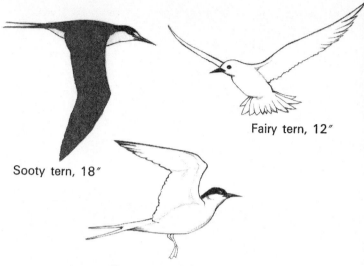

Sooty tern, 18″

Fairy tern, 12″

Roseate tern, 16″

little is known of the prenuptial flight dispersal. In the southern summer, they may be found as far south as the Weddel Sea so that in the southern oceans a wide dispersal of these birds into all regions takes place.

Other species of terns make long seasonal flights and although some birds may be found in the open ocean, they generally stay near to coastal waters. Some European *common terns* winter along the shores of west and south-west Africa, while others go to Madagascar and even as far as India. In America the common tern winters in the Mexican Gulf and the coasts of South America. Asiatic common terns may be found on the southern and eastern coasts of that continent during the northern winter. Other terns with a world-wide distribution, particularly in tropical island regions, are the *sooty*, the *roseate* and the *brown noddy*. *Fairy terns* are widely encountered in the central Pacific area.

Although terns are very difficult to catch at sea they are

Kittiwake, 16″

usually to be found in areas where small fish or shrimps abound, so that the castaway may expect to find a fairly high level of marine life where terns are seen feeding, diving in a distinctive way after their prey, and usually flying off directly they return to the surface. On land they lay single eggs in burrows or on low branches and are more easily caught.

(g) Kittiwake

The kittiwake only visits the coast during the breeding season and spends the rest of the year on the open ocean. Widely distributed around the world in the middle and high northern latitudes, they leave the high seas about June and are then observed only around their nesting places; this migration includes the younger birds which may still be too young to breed. Their return to the sea takes place from August to October and they are then distributed all over the oceans.

Red-billed tropic bird, 24½″

Masked booby, 38″

Brown booby, 38″

114

They are to be found from November to April over the North Atlantic from 60°N down to the tropics but their migration does not follow any particular pattern and may take place in a westerly as well as a southerly direction.

h) Tropic birds

Tropic birds, sometimes called *bosun birds* after the marlin-spike appearance of their tail plumage, are mainly encountered world-wide in tropical and subtropical areas, as their name suggests. Although they do not migrate they may be encountered many hundreds of miles from land and are not gregarious by nature except when nesting. Although they may circle a survival craft closely they seldom alight, and after a casual inspection continue towards their destination. They feed by diving for fish and squid.

Magnificent frigate bird, 40″

(j) Boobies

Boobies have a similar distribution to that of tropic birds and, though not migratory, may also be found many hundreds of miles from land. They are, however, extremely curious and quite fearless; they will not only approach a survival craft but will alight upon it, or even the castaways themselves, if nothing is done to frighten them away. Since they are huge birds and make good eating, they could well make a useful contribution to the castaway's diet if food is in short supply.

Gannet, 36″

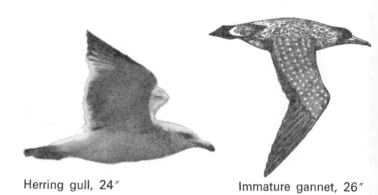

Herring gull, 24″

Immature gannet, 26″

Great black-backed gull, 29″

Common gull, 16″

(k) Frigate birds

Found mainly in tropical and subtropical island areas in the Atlantic, Pacific and Indian oceans, these birds live mostly by hunting flying fish and by marauding attacks on boobies, gannets and other sea birds, forcing them to disgorge their prey to escape attack. Like boobies and tropic birds, they may be found many hundreds of miles out into the ocean and have a seemingly unlimited capacity for remaining airborne. It is unlikely that frigate birds will approach a survival craft near enough to be caught unless they land on the sea in error and from which they find it very difficult to take off again.

(l) Gannets

Gannets have a world-wide distribution but are less venturesome in the migratory sense. Although young birds may travel 4000 miles in a coastwise direction, the adults rarely travel half that distance and usually remain within the area of the continental shelf, often close to the shore-line, feeding on schools of fish by diving into them from a height.

(m) Gulls
Herring, great black-backed

Gulls are probably the most familiar type of sea birds known to man but they are strictly coastal inhabitants and seldom venture beyond coastal waters. Some younger birds will cross the ocean but these are isolated cases. As a general rule, the gull family sticks to shallow waters, living from a wide range of marine food and scraps. They are difficult to catch unless they can be snared or caught with bait, but are quite edible if skinned. Like fish in polluted waters, they should not be eaten if there is a risk of contamination.

(2) Shore and Land Birds

Shore birds often make long migratory flights to their winter feeding grounds and their flyways often cross large stretches

Bartailed godwit, 16″

Swallow, 7½″

Brambling, 5¾″

Starling, 8½″

A pack of knots, 14″

of ocean. This list includes only the regular migratory species with this particular characteristic, for shore birds may be seen quite frequently in coastal waters, especially where land is separated by only a few hundreds of miles of sea, offering little obstacle to strong fliers.

Land birds are rarely seen over large stretches of ocean, for their migration routes are selected to cross seas where islands offer convenient stepping stones or where the narrowest channels offer least obstacle to less robust fliers. Exceptions to this rule are vagrant flights, for instance, from Northern America to Europe, which are accomplished by most unlikely species of small birds. It is thought that the birds are probably carried eastwards in the high speed 'jetstreams' of upper altitudes and that many perish en route, which would explain why many small exhausted land birds are recovered by ships in mid-ocean. It is unlikely, however, that even the less discerning of castaways would confuse these isolated recoveries with flights from a nearby land mass or a

Curlew, 23″

regular migration flight. (It is also unlikely that the exhausted vagrant will live, for starvation coupled with severe dehydration is probably the cause of its inability to remain airborne.)

Heron, 36″

(a) *Golden plover*

One of the most spectacular ocean migrants amongst the shore birds is the golden plover. From their breeding grounds in Alaska across to Siberia, they migrate to the southern hemisphere in three flyways: (a) from West Siberia through Europe to the Mediterranean; (b) from Labrador by way of a route east of Bermuda and the West Indies to south Brazil and

Cormorant, 30″

Snow-geese, 28″

Pintail, 30″

Uruguay; (c) from the Aleutians and Alaska to Hawaii, thence through the islands to New Zealand, and from eastern Siberia to the Malaysian Archipelago.

(b) Tattlers

Similar flights are performed by many varieties of the *tattler* group of shore birds (the *bristle-thighed curlew*, for example, making a non-stop flight from Alaska to Hawaii). Many varieties of *godwits, sandpipers* and their allied families of waders also perform prodigious ocean crossings on regular migratory flights. Migrations take place in the autumn months of the northern hemisphere but the return flyway in the spring does not necessarily take the same route, the group which breeds in the Canadian northland, for instance, making its way up the American mainland instead of retracing the ocean passage of the autumn.

(c) Herons

Another widely distributed species, the many types of heron, frequents coastal and inland waters as a rule but on occasion may be found making long ocean passages between islands. The many varieties include *bitterns* and *egrets*, the latter sometimes crossing long stretches of ocean although they are, like the *cattle egret*, mostly land-orientated in their feeding practices. There are quite a number of instances on record of trans-Atlantic crossings by groups of these birds, indicating that their capacity for nomadic behaviour extends well beyond coastal regions.

(d) Cormorants, geese, ducks

Waterfowl of many species are well known for their migratory character, although their migration routes generally follow land contours and do not involve long ocean passages. Spring migration takes place usually from middle to high latitudes and vice versa in autumn, both routes generally in a north-south direction. Some very long coastal flights, extending

200 or 300 miles from land, may be observed in sea areas such as the southern approaches to Korea, and from Alaska to the Pacific coasts of America. Occasional American visitors reach British shores and considerable flights take place from western Europe to Greenland and the northern Eurasian mainland. In the southern hemisphere, similar migrations take place from continental America, Africa and Australia towards the islands lying to the south of these continents.

Near the coast of the country towards which migration is taking place exhausted stragglers may be found swimming in the sea, but if the flight is of *cormorants* they will be naturally found swimming submerged to their necks, a characteristic of this species.

(e) Cuckoo

Land birds which regularly migrate across stretches of ocean are rare, but some species, mostly the cuckoo, may be found widely distributed around the islands of the South Pacific. The *long-tailed cuckoo*, a native of New Zealand, spreads throughout the vast island area stretching from the Solomon Islands to the Pitcairn Islands in a migration to winter feeding grounds. The *bronze cuckoo* migrates from New Zealand to the Solomons in March and returns in September, a long ocean passage of over 2000 miles; the Australian members of this species cross the Timor Sea to New Guinea and the islands westward.

From Madagascar also there are several species of land birds which regularly migrate to winter feeding grounds in Africa but this does not entail long ocean passages as the flights are coastal. The flyways taken by European land birds often cross the Mediterranean but are largely north to south. Species whose flight is dependent on vertical air currents cross only where the stretches of sea are narrowest.

In general, it will be seen from the foregoing examples that, during the migratory periods from March to May and from September to November, it is quite probable that shore birds of many species can be found in flight over the oceans in addition to the regular oceanic natives. That isolated flights of land birds may be sighted is also possible and no reliance may be placed on single observations to determine either the distance from land or the transit of the survival craft across a migration route. It can, however, be safely assumed that a general increase in non-migratory bird activity will be one of the first indications that a survival craft is approaching land. Unfortunately, oceanic migration routes cannot be accurately charted, for routes vary according to weather conditions as well as the separate species involved.

APPENDIX C: LIFE IN THE SEA

There are few places in the wide expanse of ocean surfaces where marine life of some sort does not exist. But, as on land, there are some areas where food is plentiful with a high incidence of life and others where, by reason of a low interchange of surface water, food is scarce and fishing poor. It is important that castaways should be able to locate the nearest areas of high density marine life, not only to improve their chances of catching food but also so that they may navigate towards an area where commercial fishing craft may be encountered.

The photographs of marine life on pages 44-45 are self-explanatory or have already been covered by the relevant chapter on fishing, and the areas of high incidence of marine life are shown on the ocean maps. It may however be of interest to those adrift on the ocean surface to have a brief explanation of the luminescence which surrounds them at night and a cautionary word about plankton and other forms of very minute life at sea.

Blue

Fin

Dolphin

Porpoise

Sei

Pilot

Humpback

Killer

Grey

Sperm

Whales (left): The killer and the sperm are predators (dangerous), the others are plankton eating (harmless). Sharks (right): The whale shark, manta ray and basking shark are plankton eating, the others are predators

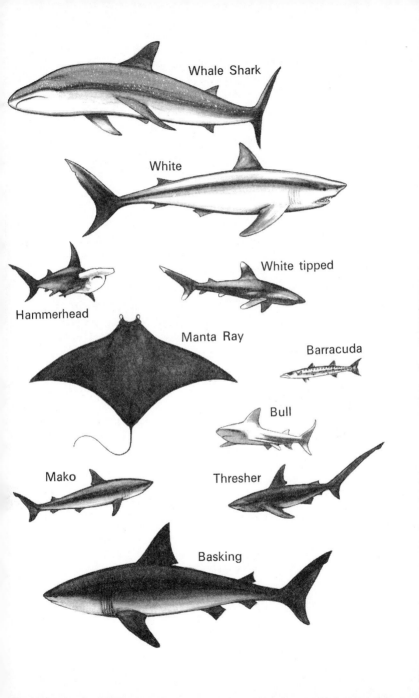

Vegetable plankton converts minerals into food through photosynthesis, and in the process gives off more oxygen than it requires, so providing for other sea animals as well. The most abundant types of vegetable plankton, called *diatoms,* are so concentrated at times of high growth rate that the sea is stained a brownish green. Another type of plankton of the vegetable type (but which may also be classified as animal) are the *flagellates.* When conditions (usually tropical) of growth permit, these organisms multiply so switly that huge areas of sea are coloured brown, red or orange and so intense is the concentration that the sea becomes de-oxygenated and all marine life in the vicinity dies from suffocation. Flagellates possess luminescent properties and, with small types of jellyfish, are responsible for a great deal of the luminescence visible in the sea at night. These two types of plankton are too small to be trapped in a small mesh net, but since they are inedible this is of no consequence. However, the larger types of *animal plankton* and small crustaceans which may be trapped in a small mesh 'plankton net' (see diagram on p. 51) can contribute to the castaways' diet, but should be taken in small quantities only after the removal of any jellyfish and larger pieces of vegetable matter.

Much of this animal plankton rises to the surface of the ocean at night-time to feed, and is absent from surface layers during the day, so that the collection of plankton is best carried out as an overnight exercise, the net being withdrawn during the day.

Larger forms of marine life such as shrimp, squid, krill and small fish, some luring with and some attracted by luminescence, may also be trapped by the net and these form useful additions to the castaways' diet. Marine life of all sizes, from turtles to whales, rely on vegetable plankton and zooplankton for their nutrients, and because of their specially adapted feeding mechanisms they are relatively harmless to humans in the predatory sense, although they can inadvertently cause damage to survival craft. In spite of their immense size, there is no reason for castaways to be afraid of plankton-eating creatures and much of the alarmist folklore connected with these 'sea-monsters' is the product of old wives' tales rather than recorded fact. The accompanying examples of plankton-eating fauna (see pp. 126-7) are therefore included as much for the castaways' peace of mind as for their interest.

APPENDIX D: NAVIGATIONAL DATA

Apart from rising and setting celestial bodies, it is possible also to find direction of travel from observations of the Pole Star, which is always within a degree of the true geographical North. If in the southern hemisphere, the Southern Cross provides a good indication of true geographical South as the top and bottom stars of the cross point to the pole's approximate position on the horizon (see star charts, pp. 133 and 134).

The declinations of moon and planets change too swiftly to include their tabulation in this section but sometimes the moon's position in the celestial sphere relates closely to the stars given in the table (see below), and when this occurs the amplitude of the brighter objects can be a useful approximation.

AMPLITUDES

(True bearings of rising and setting stars and planets)

Lat.	Declination						
	0°	5°	10°	15°	20°	25°	29°
0°	0	5	10	15	20	25	29
10°	0	5·1	10·2	15·3	20·3	25·4	29·5
20°	0	5·3	10·7	15·9	21·4	26·7	31·1
30°	0	5·8	11·6	17·4	23·3	29·2	34·1
40°	0	6·5	13·1	19·8	26·5	33·5	39·3
45°	0	8·5	14·2	21·5	28·9	36·7	43·3
50°	0	9·4	15·7	23·8	32·2	41·1	49·0
55°	0	10·5	17·6	26·8	36·6	47·5	57·7
60°	0	12·1	20·3	31·2	43·2	57·7	75·8
62½°	0	13·1	22·1	34·1	47·8	66·2	—

Latitude N or S

Bearing of object is named:
{
E when rising
W when setting
N or S according to declination
}

Example: Approximate latitude of survival craft is 45° N
June Sun's declination 23½° N
from page 132   rising bearing E 34½° N or NE×E
December Sun's declination 23½° S
from page 132   setting bearing W 34½° S or
SW×W

130

Time for observation is correct when the lower rim of the sun is a semi-diameter above the horizon thus: ___O___

In high latitudes the sun rises and sets with too much horizontal movement for accurate observation.

Recognition

Planets are easily distinguished from stars by the steady quality of their reflected light as opposed to the twinkling character of starlight.

Venus: Visible for a short time after sunset or before sunrise, has a bluish light and is the brightest of the planets.

Jupiter: Next in brilliance to Venus and much brighter than any of the fixed stars, Jupiter is easily discernible on the horizon in clear weather, when rising or setting. Both Venus and Jupiter may well be mistaken by uninformed lookout for the navigation lights of a ship.

Mars: Fluctuates in brilliance during the course of the year and is known for its reddish colour.

Saturn: Yellowish in colour, has least brilliance of these four planets and is equal in brightness to a first magnitude star.

DECLINATIONS

Mid-month	Sun	Stars	Mag.	Declination
January	21° S	Antares	1·2	26° S
February	13° S	Aldebaran*	0·2	19° N
March	2° S	Altair	1·7	6° N
April	10° N	Betelgeuse*	av. 0·5	7° N
May	19° N	Arcturus	1·1	16° N
June	23½° N	Bellatrix	0·9	9° N
July	21½° N	Procyon*	0·5	5° N
August	14° N	Rigel*	0·3	8° S
September	3° N	Sirius*	−1·6	17° S
October	8½° S	Spica	1·2	11° S
November	18½° S	Canopus*	−0·9	53° S
December	23½° S	Vega*	0·1	39° N

* Particularly bright stars.

Note. The irregular movement of planets does not allow a permanent prediction for the declination of these bodies but their celestial position may be estimated in relation to the stars at zenith.

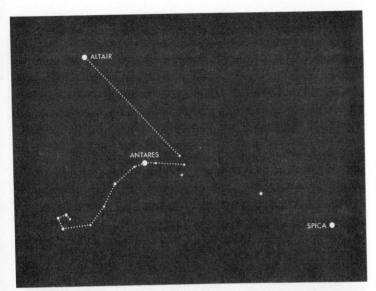

A Scorpio

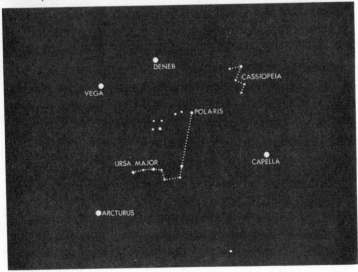

B Pole Star

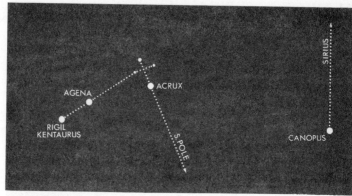

C Southern Cross

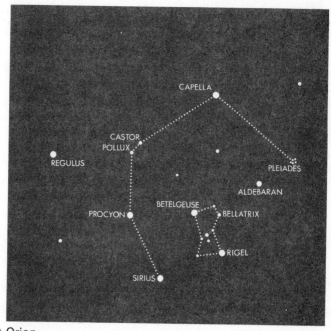

D Orion

APPENDIX E: SURVIVAL CHARTS

In the three oceanic charts, the five basic factors in survival navigation have been studied and recorded.

(1) Rainfall

Where possible, statistics for the ten-year period from 1951 to 1960 have been used to give a guide to normal rainfall levels. (Rainfall statistics are subject to considerable annual fluctuation so that these averages should not be taken as positive expectations.) The amounts for each month are registered in centimetres, to the nearest whole number, around the name of the island or station printed in the centre. The months are in rotation from January to the right of twelve o'clock, to December at the left. In ocean areas no statistics are available and I have tried to estimate the months in which survival amounts of rainfall may be expected, using 5 centimetres per month as the level above which enough rain may be collected to allow castaways to replenish supplies by reasonable means of catchment. Such months are coloured blue and the months in which less than 5 centimetres may be expected are left white but this does not necessarily mean that these months are entirely arid. Island statistics can be used in loose support of expected rainfall in sea areas nearby. Stations have been chosen for their proximity to sea level and their isolation from the higher land masses.

(2) Drift

Average seasonal wind values have been used to estimate the drift which a survival craft would experience during the summer and winter periods; this takes into account the proper management of the craft using the sea anchor and other aids to maintain stability and improve its seaworthiness in heavy weather. The drift experienced by a well sea-anchored survival craft in gale force winds has a rate similar to that of a lightly sea-anchored craft in a moderate to fresh breeze, so that the rate of drift is no indication of actual wind strength.

Drift in the direction of the black arrows is unavoidable where a © indicates that the wind blows constantly in the same direction (such as in the trade wind belts). Choice of direction may be exercised by a judicious use of the sea-anchor where an ⊗ at the arrowhead denotes that the wind direction is variable but predominantly in the direction indicated by the shaft. Crossed shafts with a circle at each end indicate that there is no predominant wind direction in the area and that progress by drift is equally possible in any chosen direction but the rate will be very slow and in such areas the set of the ocean current may well dictate the direction of travel.

Each flight at the tail of the arrow represents half a knot in the direction indicated by the shaft but progress will be improved if assisted by sailing or rowing, depending upon the type of survival craft which is available to the castaway. In most areas the drift arrow drawn on the north side of the circle represents the months October to March and on the south side of the circle for the months of April to September. The exception to this occurs in the monsoon areas where the drift arrows are based on wind directions during the north-east and south-west monsoons.

(3) Surface Ocean Currents

The average set of ocean currents is shown by the blue arrows. Annual fluctuations occur in the paths taken by established currents like the Gulf Stream and the Kuro Shio so that they are not as wide as their charted positions seem to indicate. They are, however, fairly easily detected by their considerable difference in temperature from the surrounding ocean waters or from nearby counter-currents so that the castaway will have little difficulty in determining his transit of the thermal boundary where these currents are in their well defined earlier stages. Thermal boundaries become more vague as the currents spread and mingle with static ocean waters but temperature still remains the best guide as to the direction in which the survival craft is being set. Local fluctuations in temperature occur from upwellings or from icebergs but these variations are usually of short duration or accompanied by visible phenomena.

Equatorial counter-currents have seasonal fluctuations but the boundaries of these currents may be located by a change in temperature or by the considerable eddies and upwellings which occur due to the convergence of the trade drift.

The arrows carry red circles to denote warm currents and blue circles for cold currents where these are juxtaposed. Current arrows change their colour to white where they cross the blue of the rainfall circles. The rate of the current in knots is given in blue numbers for the area in which it is situated.

(4) Inhabited Coasts
These are coloured yellow and have been included to indicate to the castaway the areas where he may find help after he has landed. In order to find assistance in landing it would be necessary to navigate the survival craft along the inhabited coast until a village was reached where a good landing area would be likely. In calmer weather it is easier to travel along the coast in the survival craft than to try to walk, especially after a long and difficult ordeal.

(5) Magnetic Variation
Green variation lines are at 10° intervals except where a 5° line has been introduced to clarify the gradient. Although the

annual fluctuation may amount to 1/5th° either way (change is greatest nearer the poles) these values (which are for the year 1970) are quite suitable for use in survival navigation up to the year 1990.

ROUTE CHART

Admiralty chart No. 3934 has been used as a base to illustrate the following information.

(1) Continental Shelf Areas

Sea areas with a depth of less than 1000 fathoms which are also associated with land masses or islands are white except where they are overlaid with the colour of a bird migration route. All other sea areas are coloured blue.

(2) Density of Marine Life

Ocean areas in which marine life is plentiful enough to attract commercial fishing fleets are hatched in white and bordered with a white broken line. All sea areas within the continental shelf, particularly in depths of less than 100 fathoms, have high fish populations and fishing fleets may be found working anywhere in these regions.

Ocean areas where fish are scarce have been given a tonal value of black dots. Commercial fishing vessels are unlikely to be encountered in these waters except when they are crossing them to reach a fishing zone.

All other sea areas have enough fish to attract occasional tuna fishing craft, especially within the regions inhabited by flying fish (latitude 30° N to 30° S approximately) or where the seabed lies within 100 fathoms of the surface. (Tuna long-liners stream buoyed fishing lines up to 7 miles in length.)

(3) Bird Migration

Migration routes originating in the nothern hemisphere are coloured pink, those originating in the southern hemisphere are orange. These routes are not rigidly followed by the species which are listed at the source and many divergences take place, for instance, when storms occur along the established routes. Land and shore species adhere more rigidly to established routes than do birds which live from the oceans. Short arrows denote species which migrate as individuals to warmer areas as the season demands (kittiwakes, fulmars, albatrosses, giant petrels, etc) and a note referring to the limits within which they usually range is placed near their breeding sites. Species which follow longer routes (shearwaters, Wilson's petrels, terns, etc.) migrate in flocks to summer feeding areas where they disperse for a few months before reassembling to return to their breeding grounds. Where return routes are not illustrated the species concerned either follows the same route back, especially where it depends on areas of dense marine life for food, or, in the case of land and shore species which undertake direct flights, the return route tends to lie to the westward of the outward migration. Good examples of this may be found in the return routes of the golden plover and associated species which, in the Pacific, travel northwards along a route which directly crosses Wake Island, 1000 miles to the west, or in the Atlantic where the return route (illustrated) runs directly up the land mass of Central and North America. Return migrations of the Arctic tern in the Atlantic, during the northern spring, take place up the eastern seaboard of South and North America as well as on the routes followed by the outward migration. Non-migratory species of seabirds which are sometimes encountered far from land are listed in the margins of the tropical zones.

No reliance may be placed on bird migration for navigational purposes, but castaways should expect to see some form of oceanic bird life around them and a familiarity with the species concerned will enable them to realise the significance of any new sightings or whether an increase in numbers is due to the proximity of land or simply that the craft is transiting a migration route.

Migrations which are largely coastal, such as those undertaken by waterfowl and their associated species, have been omitted to avoid congestion.

(4) Tropical Revolving Storms

Areas where such storms develop are denoted by black arrows mostly around latitude 10° north or south of the equator. The circulation of the coil outwards from the centre gives the direction of the wind circulation of the storms in each hemisphere: examples of subsequent tracks are indicated by black arrows. The months in which they are most likely to occur are noted at the point of origin.

(5) Shipping Routes

Principal great circle routes, with modifications for bad weather zones, which are used by ocean shipping are illustrated in green. Straight lines should be drawn between relevant major ports to find the survival craft's proximity to the shorter shipping routes. The considerable distortions associated with Mercator's projection in high latitudes must be taken into account when estimating distances in these regions.

INDEX

References in bold type indicate illustrations

144

146